WOMEN
IN THE
THIRD
WORLD

WOMEN
IN THE
THIRD WORLD

MAXINE P. FISHER

FRANKLIN WATTS
NEW YORK / LONDON / TORONTO
SYDNEY / 1989

13, /25

Photographs courtesy of: Reuters/Bettmann Newsphotos: pp. 8, 139; Impact Visuals: pp. 11 (Orde Eliason), 35 and 36 (Kathleen Foster), 51 and 74 (Amy Zuckerman), 87 (top, Sue Dorfman), 100 (Cindy Reiman); Monkmeyer: pp. 20 (Mimi Forsyth), 24 (both; top, Hays), 27 (Tim Gidal), 53 (Mimi Forsyth), 56 (Arlene Collins), 69 (Rameshwar Das), 85 (Willem Van de Poll), 97 (Mimi Forsyth), 109 (Arlene Collins), 122 (P. Boucas for WHO), 131 (Chapelle), 146 (Paul Conklin), 148 (Russell Dian); Liaison: pp. 30 (Jean Claude Francolon), 45 (both; bottom, Katie Arkaau), 152 (Pascal Maitre); UPI/Bettmann Newsphotos: pp. 63, 96, 157; UN Photo: pp. 87 (bottom, P.S. Sudhakaran), 106 (John Isaac).

Library of Congress Cataloging-in-Publication Data

Fisher, Maxine P., 1948–

Women in the Third World / by Maxine P. Fisher.
p. cm.
Bibliography: p.
Includes index.
Summary: Examines the lifestyles of women born and raised in developing nations, focusing on their education, employment, marriage, and family life.
ISBN 0-531-10666-7
1. Women—Developing countries—Social conditions—Juvenile literature. 2. Poor women—Developing countries—Juvenile literature. [1. Women—Developing countries—Social conditions. 2. Developing countries—Social conditions.] I. Title.
HQ1870.9.F57 1989   88-31649 CIP AC
305.4'09172'4—dc19

CONTENTS

For Mom and Dad

*Many grateful thanks
to Sophie Tran-Dinh*

Frontis: *Two Egyptian students walk outside the university in Cairo. It is part of their Islamic religion that women wear veils in public.*

1
THE THIRD WORLD

There has been a lot of talk in recent years about the Third World. But exactly what and where is it?

"The Third World" is a phrase used mostly by scholars and journalists. Some use it simply to refer to countries marked by extreme poverty, as is done in this book. For others the term refers to the politically nonaligned countries of the world—those without permanent alliances with either the United States or the Soviet Union. The United Nations uses the term "developing countries."

Recently some scholars have even begun to speak of this country's black, Hispanic, and Native American populations as Third World Americans. It is a legitimate label since it reminds us that here in the United States, historically impoverished ethnic groups face many of the same problems as people in countries we tend to regard as quite different from ours.

But this book is not about America's poor. It is about women who were born and raised in relatively poor countries. The statistics on this population paint an appalling picture. The rates of adult illiteracy are extremely high, as are the rates of infant and maternal mortality. In many parts of Africa almost half of the rural women are managing farms and households without the aid of a husband. The men have moved elsewhere in search of wage labor, so these women depend on the help of children. Indeed, in many of the poor countries of the world children are greatly valued not only for emotional reasons, but also for the work they do while they are still youngsters, as well as for the support they may provide in the future when parents can no longer work.

Adult women of the Third World have had a grim life, but there are indications that their daughters may fare better. Some important changes have occurred recently, partly as a result of the United Nations (U.N.) Decade For Women (1975–1985), which stimulated governments to redefine work in such a way that women's contributions to national economies are now being recorded and thus officially acknowledged. This in turn has made women farmers eligible for the technical assistance that has long been denied them. The U.N. conferences also encouraged the gathering of data on problems facing women around the world. Perhaps most importantly, female literacy increased markedly during the decade with the implication that female youngsters will be less disadvantaged in the job market years from now.

Emigration from the Third World to the highly developed Western countries has accelerated during the past quarter of a century, among both those seeking higher education and those seeking employment. A number of women who were born and raised in Third World countries but who are now studying or working in the United States are profiled in the following pages. Although not

An Indian woman, living on the outskirts of Delhi, hangs her washing under the watchful eye of one of her family's cattle.

Third World Countries

Afghanistan
Algeria
Angola
Antigua
Argentina
Bahamas
Bahrain
Bangladesh
Barbados
Belize
Benin
Bhutan
Bolivia
Botswana
Brazil
Brunei
Burkina Faso
    (formerly Upper Volta)
Burma
Burundi
Cameroon
Cape Verde
Central African Republic
Chad
Chile
Colombia
Comoros
Congo
Costa Rica
Cuba
Djibouti
Dominica
Dominican Republic

Ecuador
Egypt
El Salvador
Equatorial Guinea
Ethiopia
Fiji
Gabon
Ghana
Grenada
Guatemala
Guinea
Guinea-Bissau
Guyana
Haiti
Honduras
India
Indonesia
Iran
Iraq
Ivory Coast
Jamaica
Jordan
Kampuchea
    (formerly Cambodia)
Kenya
Kiribati
Korea (South)
Korea (North)
Kuwait
Laos
Lebanon
Lesotho
Liberia

Libya
Madagascar
Malawi
Malaysia
Maldives
Mali
Mauritania
Mauritius
Mexico
Morocco
Mozambique
Nauru
Nepal
Nicaragua
Niger
Nigeria
Oman
Pakistan
Panama
Papua New Guinea
Paraguay
Peru
Phillipines
Qatar
Rwanda
St. Kitts & Nevis
St. Lucia
St. Vincent
Sao Tome & Principe
Saudi Arabia
Senegal

Seychelles
Sierra Leone
Singapore
Solomon Islands
Somalia
Sri Lanka
Sudan
Surinam
Swaziland
Syria
Tanzania
Thailand
Togo
Tonga
Trinidad & Tobago
Tunisia
Turkey
Tuvalu
Uganda
United Arab Emirates
Uruguay
Vanuatu
Venezuela
Vietnam
Western Samoa
Yemen Arab Republic
Yemen Democratic
  Republic (Southern)
Zaire
Zambia
Zimbabwe

Source: Encyclopedia of the Third World, George Thomas Kurian, ed. (New York: Facts on File, 1978, 1987)

Atlantic
Ocean

Union of Soviet
Socialist Republics
(USSR)

E U R O P E

BLACK SEA

MEDITERRANEAN SEA

PERSIAN
GULF

Morocco

Tunisia

Algeria

Libya

Egypt

Western
Sahara

RED SEA

Djibouti

ARABIAN
SEA

Senegal

Mauritania

Mali

Niger

Chad

Sudan

GULF OF ADEN

Gambia

Burkina Faso
(Upper Volta)

Nigeria

Cen. Afr.
Rep.

Uganda

Ethiopia

Somali Rep

Guinea

Benin

Guinea-Bissau

Togo

Cameroon

Congo

Rwanda

Kenya

Indian
Ocean

Liberia

Ghana

Zaire

Ivory Coast

Equatorial
Guinea

Burundi

Tanzania

Sierra Leone

Gabon

Malawi

Mozambique

Angola

Zambia

Mozambique
Channel

Madagascar

Namibia

Zimbabwe

Botswana

Transvaal

So.
Africa

Swaziland

Natal

Lesotho

Africa and Europe

Union of Soviet Socialist Republics
(USSR)

BLACK SEA

Turkey

Syria

Lebanon
Israel

Jordan

Iraq

Kuwait

Iran

Persian
Gulf

Saudi
Arabia

Yemen
South Yemen

RED SEA

Gulf of Aden

Oman

Afghanistan

Pakistan

India

Nepal

China

Mongolia

South
Korea

North
Korea

Japan

EAST CHINA SEA

Bangladesh

Burma

Bay
of
Bengal

Laos

Taiwan
(Formosa)

Vietnam
Cambodia
(Kampuchea)

Philippines

SO. CHINA SEA

Thailand

Sri Lanka

Singapore

Sumatra

Java

Brunei

Malaysia

Indonesia

Papua New Guinea

ARABIAN SEA

Mozambique Channel

Indian
Ocean

Australia

Asia and the Middle East

Canada

United States

Atlantic Ocean

Mexico

GULF OF MEXICO

CARIBBEAN SEA

Jamaica

Haiti

Cuba

Dom. Republic

Belize

Honduras

Puerto Rico

Guatemala

Nicaragua

Barbados

El Salvador

Venezuela

Guyana

Costa Rica

Suriname

Panama

Colombia

Fr. Guiana

Ecuador

Peru

Brazil

Pacific Ocean

Bolivia

Paraguay

Argentina

Uruguay

Chile

North, Central and South America

typical of the vast majority of their impoverished compatriots, they can nonetheless teach us something about their countries.

Many but not all of these countries have only recently acquired their independence from colonial powers. In some of these areas, notably in West Africa, it appears that the colonial experience resulted in a decrease in the status of women. This is important to bear in mind for we tend to think of the modern West, and the United States in particular, as the fountainhead of feminism. In West Africa women are currently struggling to attain a degree of economic independence and esteem that belonged to their great-grandmothers in the days of their tribal past.

How large is the Third World? According to the *Encyclopoedia of the Third World*, in 1978, 118 member nations of the U.N. were also countries of the Third World, making up half the land surface in the world and containing half the world's people. Sixty percent of Third World inhabitants live in poverty—about 1.2 billion people. Forty Third World countries are the world's poorest.

If the Third World is this vast, clearly it is important to learn something of its people. It is hoped that this book fairly represents the lives of some of its female members, and that the courage, pluck, and fortitude they show will be a source of enduring inspiration.

BEING BORN FEMALE

She was a girl who arrived when everyone was expecting a boy. So since she was such a disappointment to her parents, to her immediate family, to her tribe, nobody thought of recording her birth. She was so insignificant.

from *Second Class Citizen*
by Buchi Emecheta

When a girl was born in the hospital, Tunde tried to hide his joy and pretend to have preferred a boy. His wife Laide smiled and told him she was not fooled.

from *The Chief*
by Alice Hellyer Dally

The words quoted above are from works of fiction, but they are works closely drawn from real life. Both books were written by living novelists describing roughly the same time and place: rural Nigeria in the years following World War II. Taken together, these two scenes remind us of two things. The first is that the birth of a baby is greeted differently depending on whether it is a boy or a girl. The second is that people do not always react to an event according to custom.

Throughout most of recorded history in much of the world the sex of an infant makes a lasting difference to its family. And almost everywhere this is so, boys are preferred. Although this preference is probably as prevalent in developed countries as in developing ones, and definitely so in certain ethnic groups, discrimination against girls in Third World countries is greater and in some cases even cruel.

Traditionally, the difference in attitude toward boy versus girl was shown in Third World countries as soon as the child was born. One way was in the kind and amount of ritual ceremonies preformed just after the birth. Typically the birth ceremonies for boys included a big party.

This is still true of the Bedouins of the Middle East. These are nomadic desert-dwelling people who live for the most part by herding flocks of sheep, goats, and camels. They regard the birth of a boy as an event worthy of a grand feast. Many people are invited, and the celebration goes on for days. As part of the festivities—and in order to feed all the guests—the family to whom the child has been born slaughters one of the animals from their herd. This is something done only on the most special occasions, for the Bedouins depend for their livelihood on the milk produced by their beasts, which is sold or bartered for desperately needed goods. When a daughter is born the family does not slaughter an animal. Nor do they throw a party. On the contrary, the husband and wife are consoled by their relatives, who hope aloud that the next pregnancy will produce a son.[1]

When a male child is born in northern India, the village women still gather to sing it songs of welcome to the world. If it's a female, there's a telling silence. But not long ago in this part of the world, a woman's in-laws would think nothing of hurling abuse at her for giving birth to a girl. They would add that this was a sure sign she would bring bad luck to her new family.[2]

Throughout rural India, Hindus pray that the birth of a son be followed by still more sons. One prayer adds: "The birth of a girl, grant it elsewhere, here grant a son."[3] Rit-

uals, too, are preformed to ensure that a woman bears a son. One of them aims to magically change the sex of the fetus if it happens to already be a girl.

Formerly in many places where land was the major source of wealth, people often resorted to female infanticide, the practice of killing girl babies, because in agricultural societies where women move in with their husbands' families upon marriage, people are likely to look upon sons as an investment with high returns but daughters as a burdensome expense. This is because a family must support a daughter while she is growing up, bear the considerable cost of her wedding, and then lose her labor to another family when she marries and moves away. Sons, on the other hand, are seen as earning their keep. They stay put, contribute their adult years of labor to their own families, and take care of their aging parents. Or so the parents hope.

In this century the practice of female infanticide has taken a more subtle form. Girl babies are far less likely to be killed outright. But in some places, there is a tendency for families to provide young daughters with less food and inferior health care than they give sons.

In Khalapur, North India, for example, in the 1960s twice as many girls as boys died before reaching maturity because they received inferior medical attention. Families took boys to the hospital when the need arose. With girls they waited far longer, sometimes too long to save their lives.[4] And a 1983 study of 236 children under the age of

An Indian girl in Calcutta. In India, boys are preferred to girls because girls are considered a financial burden on their families.

five in two villages of West Bengal showed that although malnutrition of children of both sexes was extremely high, the girls in both villages "are systematically more undernourished at every level."[5]

Rural India is not the only place where there is family pressure to neglect daughters. The Egyptian writer Nawal El Saadawi speaks of the same problem in her country.[6] Around the world, however, attitudes are beginning to change, although the reasons for the change are not always encouraging. One important factor is the tremendous amount of migration that has taken place in recent decades throughout the Third World.

Today in Africa, in the Caribbean, and in Latin America, husbands and wives often find themselves living in different regions, sometimes different countries. Young women, like those employed in the strawberry-packing industry in Mexico, are finding they must work because funds from a distantly settled husband are insufficient to support children. In most instances it is the job market that is responsible for separating families. But in any case, women are increasingly earning wages for their labor and being recognized as supporters of families. Daughters frequently also take on the responsibility of caring for their aged relatives—male and female, in-laws as well as blood kin.

With the belated recognition of adult female contributions of support comes the idea that female babies must be valued. We have yet to see this new attitude translated into new female birth ceremonies, but it is emerging nevertheless. In African cities, for example, women working in the marketplaces realize that most likely it will be their grown daughters, not their sons, who will assist them in their efforts to gain an income and in later years to take care of them. As a result such women are now saying they prefer to have daughters, a confession their not-too-distant ancestors would have found shocking.

GROWING UP

Fatiha wanted to teach her young sister-in-law to read and write. But Aicha, the little girl's mother and Fatiha's powerful mother-in-law, was dead set against it. So,

> they organized their little conspiracy; it was decided to mask the reading and writing with sewing lessons. Aicha wanted this because sewing was indispensable and the more you knew in this field the better. . . . It was not the knowledge of the reading and writing that Aicha opposed, but rather the consequence this knowledge had on women.[1]

These words are from the novel *A Wife For My Son*, by Algerian writer and filmmaker Ali Ghalem. But the situation is real, not fictional. Attitudes like Aicha's have shaped the lives of millions of women throughout the developing world. Only in recent years has it become possible to see the results of a slowly shifting opinion. One shining reflection of the new attitude are school attendance records for girls. These show that nearly everywhere the percentage of girls allowed to attend primary school is climbing.

In much of the Third World the idea that only boys ought to take advantage of even primary school training long held sway. Girls, it was felt, were better served by

staying at home where at mother's side they would learn the skills thought to make them good wives and mothers themselves. As a result, as recently as the 1970s, adult female literacy was extremely low in many countries. In the rural villages of eastern Turkey, for example, almost half the adult female population could not read.[2] In Africa, where literacy rates are the lowest in the world, only 18 percent of adult women could read in 1970, but the figure rose to 27 percent by 1980.[3] This is a remarkable achievement for one decade, but in Africa the adult female population is still 30 percent less literate than adult males.

In the towns and cities of Africa, Asia, and Latin America, learning to be a good wife and mother means learning to do housework, rear children, and acquire marketing skills. In rural settings it also means working on the land. But unless she comes from an affluent family, a girl begins to work at a very early age indeed.

The rest of this chapter tells something about growing up female in four Third World countries. All the countries are relatively poor but, as you will see, the social status of women varies among them, and even within them.

Growing Up Bedouin

The Bedouins, you will remember, are the desert-dwelling nomadic people of the Middle East. Until twenty years ago, the daily routine of Bedouins of both sexes was much the same as it had been for generations.[4] Everything depended on the milk provided by their herds of sheep, goats,

Traditionally, education is reserved for boys in much of the Third World. All-male classes in the Middle East (above) and Africa (below).

and camels. From this milk, mothers and daughters would together make butter, cheese, and yogurt, major items of Bedouin trade.

During the past two decades much has changed, but the Bedouins still rely on goats for their livelihood. To an uninformed outsider, it looks almost as if the animals subsist on air; they browse contentedly on the occasional stubble found in the barren desertlike areas bordering farming communities. But the view is deceptive. These animals need pasturage, and the land available for this purpose shifts with the seasons. As a result, at least twice a year the Bedouins of Syria and Lebanon must migrate along with their herds to distant, though traditionally used, lands.

Such journeys—usually undertaken by several related households together—require them to make camp many times. And so, not surprisingly, the Bedouins were among the first people to invent the mobile home—in their case it is a big black tent. Just about everything having to do with the tent, from its manufacture to its dismantling and repair, is the concern of women and girls. Woe to the male who tries to interfere! Learning tentcraft and tent ways is a major occupation of Bedouin girls.

In a way this learning begins in early childhood, for one of the most striking things about a Bedouin tent is the amount of sexual segregation one finds inside it. There are two main divisions of the space. One area is normally occupied exclusively by adult men, although this is also the place where family meals are served and visitors entertained. In another area one usually finds the women when they are not outdoors. This is where the meals are prepared. Infants and toddlers of both sexes spend most of their time in the women's quarters.

When they are a bit older, boys and girls are expected to do small chores, such as collecting firewood. They do the same sorts of tasks, and often brothers and sisters do these together. But all this changes drastically when they reach the age of seven or eight. Then brothers give orders; sisters obey them.

A generation ago, teenage Bedouin boys and girls inhabited very different social worlds. The boys spent much of their time learning from the men how to herd animals, even spending nights alone outdoors with the flocks. They also learned how important decisions were made by the group of adult male kin, decisions that affected the whole family and its relations with its neighbors.

A Bedouin boy watches and learns from his father and other Bedouin men. In Bedouin society, the tasks such as herding animals and making important decisions are strictly men's work.

The girls, on the other hand, were mostly to be found indoors, except for the time they were milking animals or caring for a sick beast. They were learning from their mother and aunts how to spin and weave the strips that go into the construction of a tent, repair its ropes, and adjust the ropes in accordance with changes in the wind. They learned, too, how to weave carpets (a traditional Bedouin wedding gift), grind flour, and make butter and yogurt. Just as importantly, they were learning the qualities thought to make them good marriage partners.

Like girls throughout the Muslim world, these Bedouin teenagers learned that while their brothers could laugh and shout at the top of their lungs any time, they must keep their voices low, at least in public. And while their brothers could move their bodies freely without thought, they had to drop their glance wherever a male who was not a relative came into view. Deftly they would also draw a shawl across the face as modesty required.

By the time she was thirteen, a girl was under close surveillance, especially by her brothers. Whether younger or older than she, they saw themselves as her protectors. What were they protecting her from? Other men. As in other Muslim societies, the honor of a Bedouin family rests to a great extent on the virginity of its adolescent daughters. If an unmarried woman gives birth, it is her brothers and the other male members of her family who bear a large portion of the "disgrace." Small wonder then that families seek early marriage for their daughters.

The fear of losing the family honor in the form of their daughters' virginity is also related to the practice known as *purdah*—keeping women physically separate from men who are not related to them. Even in the public domain of major cities, aspects of *purdah* are still being practiced. In Saudi Arabia, for example, buses are equipped with a special walled-off section in the rear reserved for female passengers, who enter through a back door. In 1985, Saudi women protested this form of segregation by refusing to pay fares.[5]

If, traditionally, the tent was the Bedouins' mobile home, then the camel was their van. The women and children would pile onto the back of the beast among the household furnishings. Then in the company of other families similarly equipped, off they would go until it was time to make camp for the night. But eventually no camel, however accommodating, could compete with the genuine article—a mechanized vehicle.

In the mid-1960s, some Bedouin groups in Lebanon decided to sell their camels and purchase trucks with the money they got for them. Ten years later the men and boys of those groups were still delighted about the decision. The trucks had given them new-found mobility and free time. But their female relatives, who were not allowed to drive, were less than enthusiastic. The change from camel to truck had affected their lives in a rather different way.

No one can deny that migrating by truck is faster and easier than using camelpower. A trip that used to take a family weeks can now be made in half a day. But using the vehicle ties a family to roads and roadside campsites. As a result, the Bedouins have lost the chance to sell their dairy products to people living in remote areas, places once traversed by camels. Nor can they make badly needed income from the hire of extra camels, as they once did, now that the camels are gone.

How have the Bedouins made up for all this lost income? Migrating families now send their young daughters out as day laborers in the agricultural fields near where they camp. There the girls work from sunrise to mid-afternoon. When they return, it is to help carry water, sweep out the tent, and care for younger siblings. They do not attend school.

Who is to say what constitutes progress? When asked

to compare the old life-style with the new one, one Bedouin woman who had grown up in the days of the camel spoke nostalgically of the "easy life" of those times. Asked to explain what was so easy about life back then, she replied that when the women and girls of a household worked together, "work was like entertainment."[6]

Growing Up Indian

If you had been born a girl in India, your childhood would have been rather different depending on whether you were born in the countryside or in a big city, whether your family was well-to-do or poor, and whether you had many brothers or were one of many daughters.

If, like the vast majority of the Indian population today, you'd been born in a rural village, chances are that you would grow up in a household that included not only your parents and siblings, but also your father's parents; your father's unmarried sisters; his brothers (single as well as married); and finally the wives and children of his married brothers. In other words, you would be surrounded by grandparents, aunts and uncles, and a bunch of cousins— all related to you through your father.

Before your birth, all of the adults fervently hoped that you would be a boy. However, once you arrived as a girl, there was a fair chance that you'd be treated with no less affection. If you were one of many daughters born to a poor family, your relatives would bemoan the fact that

A Bedouin mother and her young children leading their camel packed with the family's belongings. Bedouin women's faces are almost completely covered.

they must begin saving for yet another dowry, the sum of money and pile of goods given by a bride's family on the occasion of her marriage.

On the whole, it would have been an indulgent infancy. You would have been in close contact with your mother, or one of the other adult females of the household, at all times. You would never have been left completely alone. When your mother went into the rice or wheat fields to work, she would have taken you along, carrying you on her hip and then putting you in a sling made from an old *sari* (an Indian dress). She'd then tie the contraption to a tree where she could keep an eye on you while she planted or weeded. At home she and the other household women would spend a good deal of time bathing and massaging you with oils, singing to you, and rocking you in a crib. You wouldn't need to cry long to gain attention. You might have cuddled up to your father or uncles as they sat in groups with their male friends, but that was only until you were about five. After that you felt funny about it.

By then you were wearing a dress and, on special occasions, cosmetics and bangle bracelets, too. You were expected to take an interest in the women's daily work. Soon you could be seen practicing balancing a water pot on your head. (Even today rural women and girls must transport well water in a heavy brass or earthen pot atop their heads.) You'd watch the activities of the women at work in the kitchen as they prepared the family meals. One day you would try pushing the heavy grinding stone in its circular path in an attempt to offer a helping hand.

In most parts of India, all children are eligible for free elementary schooling, but if you were a girl born in a rural area prior to the 1980s, you probably didn't attend. In 1977, anthropologist Doranne Jacobson reported that "many village boys attend classes, but relatively few village girls do so. 'What's the sense of teaching a girl to read and write? A woman's work is cooking and grinding' is a commonly expressed sentiment, reflected in the all-India literacy rate of 29 percent for males and 8.5 percent for females. Furthermore, some villagers believe that an educated woman will be cursed by bad fortune—barrenness, widowhood, or at the very least, dissatisfaction with traditional life."[7]

If, however, you were a girl born to a middle-class family in a big city like Bombay or Calcutta, by the age of five or six, you would be learning not one but two alphabets. Your mother—or one of your aunts if you lived in a traditional household with many aunts—would teach you and your brothers and sisters and cousins the beginnings of both English and the family's own traditional language. More than twenty distinct languages are spoken in India. Later when you attended school, you might have to learn to read and write in a third language, Hindi—the national language—and perhaps even a fourth, Sanskrit—comparable to Latin in Western schooling.

At the same time that your female country cousins were beginning to shy away from adult male relatives, your relationship with your father also changed, though in a different direction. You used to enjoy only brief, affectionate encounters; now that you have started school you spend a lot of time together. Each evening there is the serious business of his correcting your two to three hours' worth of homework.

In the cities of India one can still find traditional households—a set of brothers living together with their wives and children—but they are becoming less common. Job opportunities force many people to migrate to areas far from their kin, even to emigrate to other countries. Yet despite the difficulties and drawbacks of maintaining the traditional joint household—lack of privacy, for instance—it still remains the ideal for many Indians. Even when they settle in places far from home, brothers like to take their wives and children for a month-long visit to the household of each brother on a regular basis. This means that a man with four brothers living in far-flung cities can expect—within the course of a year or two—that each of them, along with their families, will descend on his household as guests for several weeks. But he does not consider this a problem. The burden of their accommodation and entertainment falls largely on his wife and daughters.

For a girl this means that at any given time there is likely to be a number of adult women in her household to study for glimpses into her own future. What does she see?

From her earliest days she sees her grandmother chanting and performing her daily devotions before the household shrine. Here in a nook of one of the rooms are brightly colored pictures and costumed effigies of some of the Hindu gods and goddesses. Her grandmother presents them with regular offerings of food and flowers as well as prayer. Less often—perhaps once a week—the little girl may be expected to accompany her grandmother to the local temple where, amid the heady fragrance of flowers and incense, she and the other elderly women chant and meditate.

The stories of the gods and goddesses are the first that a young Indian girl comes to know. She will find their messages more potent than the temple perfumes. They will linger longer and permeate her adult life. When the little girl is able to read, her grandmother will ask her to read aloud from the *Ramayana*, the book which describes the adventures of Sita. This legendary Indian princess was abducted from her husband by a demon king. Because she remained faithful to the end, she is considered the perfect Indian wife.

The Hindu religious calendar is full of days devoted to rituals aimed at getting good husbands for adolescent girls. In Bengal, for example, teenage girls fast on a particular day and in the evening go to a temple where they offer food and gifts to the god Síva. Because Síva is a god with a reputation for being faithful to his wife, they pray that they may be blessed with a husband just like him. Indian scholar Manisha Roy notes: "Even girls living in Calcutta and attending college believe in such observances."[8] But not all of them look upon Síva, so aloof and severe, as the ideal husband. One teenager remarked that she would prefer to perform the rituals if it would bring her a husband more like her favorite movie star!

Indian girls growing up in middle-class, urban homes also have many opportunities to observe their female relatives relax together. A young girl is not allowed to participate in the regular afternoon gatherings of her mother, her aunts, and their friends, except perhaps to greet the guests and serve them snacks. But as a teenager she can join in as they laugh, talk of mutual friends, confide in one another, and listen to radio shows aimed at women like themselves.

A music class in an all-girl Indian school

Indian girls in a science lab

The members of this all-female group will not teach our teenage girl the so-called "facts of life." That knowledge will more likely come from friends at school. But they will form a kind of support group in the bewildering process of preparing for marriage, a goal that is taken for granted.

The family may decide at this time to give their daughter singing or sitar lessons. (The sitar is a musical instrument.) But their intention in doing so is to increase her value in the marriage market, not to encourage her to become a professional musician. If a girl from such a family wishes to go to college, she will most probably be sent to a school in the same town and continue to live at home. If this is not possible, she may room at a dormitory.

In any case, daughters, unlike sons, are not generally

pressured by their families to do well at college. In the family's view, the purpose of higher education for daughters is to increase their desirability as wives, not necessarily to prepare them for a career. As a result, they may study whatever they please regardless of the subject's potential for bringing in an income. Says one young Indian woman now studying in the United States: "My cousin *had* to be a doctor or an engineer. The family pushed him very hard on this. As for me, if I wanted to be a doctor, that was fine with my father. But I didn't have to be one if I didn't want to. I was free to study anything, anything. Even sociology!"

Growing Up Ethiopian

Few girls growing up in Ethiopia in northern Africa can aspire to go to college because of that country's great lack of higher educational facilities for men or women. Ethiopian women are especially disadvantaged according to a 1982 UNICEF study. Among the reasons cited were the tradition of marrying girls at an early age, the customs preventing women from inheriting land, and the time-consuming labor performed by the women of the rural areas. But the study also mentioned the exception: "However, women in central Ethiopian cultures (Amhara, Tigré, Oromo) enjoy economic rights equal to those of men. They may inherit, sell, or buy property, and engage in business. . . . Together the Tigré and closely related Amhara ethnic groups make up 35 percent of the total population. Yet they dominate the country politically, culturally, and linguistically."[9] (Over 70 languages and 200 dialects are spoken in Ethiopia.)

Profile: Almeza

Almeza, a graduate student who now studies in the United States, comes from a family in which two powerful Ethiopian cultural groups, Amhara and Tigré, have intermarried.

She was born in 1952 in Addis Ababa, the capital city of Ethiopia. About 90 percent of the city's population lives in slums and squatter settlements, but Almeza's family lived in a comfortable spacious house. Her father, a government civil servant, was of the Tigré people. His family still lived in rural Tigré land hundreds of miles to the north. His first language was Tigrenia. Almeza's mother was of the Amhara people, who regard themselves as the founders of Ethiopia. Her language is Amharic, the country's national language and the one most spoken in Almeza's household. In the course of growing up she and her brothers and sisters also learned the language of her father's kin. In fact, Almeza learned it so well that her paternal relatives used to frequently tease her that it was a sign she was going to marry a man from her father's people.

The house in the city belonged to Almeza's mother. She inherited it from her father. It was a relatively large house, with four bedrooms and separate quarters for the domestic help. Surrounding it was a fenced-in garden. Still there were times when it didn't seem large enough, for the household itself was at times a small community.

Almeza was the third oldest child. After her came a younger sister, then two younger brothers. Two older sisters did not live in the same household. Following her peoples' custom, Almeza's mother had sent her first-born child, in this case a girl, to be reared by her own parents. This custom is found in many parts of the world. In countries where there are no nursing homes for the aged, it makes a lot of sense. Older people can have the pleasure of having a child about, and later the care and companionship of one they have in turn cared for. Almeza's mother also sent her second daughter to be raised by her parents because the child had a fiery temper. She thought her own mother might be more successful in making her happy.

Almeza's maternal grandparents lived in another quarter

of the city. She saw them and her two older sisters regularly. She recalls that the best times were holidays such as Easter when her grandmother would prepare a huge feast and all the cousins would gather at a single, long table.

In her own household there were—in addition to herself, her parents, and her three younger siblings—a number of live-in servants. Also in residence were cousins from the countryside, sent by their parents to avail themselves of the greater educational opportunities in the city. These were the youngsters on whom the parents pinned their greatest hopes. This was the only way to ensure that their children got a good primary and secondary school education.

The elementary school near where Almeza lived was an English-speaking one. As a result, she and the other children who lived in the household received their formal schooling in English. Her two older sisters, on the other hand, lived near a French-speaking school; they became fluent in the French language.

Early on, Almeza also learned traditional wifely tasks such as cleaning and cooking. "My brothers considered any kind of kitchen work insulting," she recalls. "And it was always the girls who had to make their beds and clean up after them. . . . At school girls were required to take home economics from elementary school straight through high school. We were taught knitting, weaving, sewing, and cooking while the boys took extra gym classes."

The years of home economics courses were, of course, to prepare the girls for a career in the home. And in fact many of Almeza's female classmates married after finishing the eighth grade. But Almeza came from an unusual household in one respect, and there was no family pressure on her to settle down. Quite the contrary.

As a boy of eight, her father had run away from the cattle station where he had been born. He knew that by doing so, he would greatly anger his father, a Coptic priest. (The Coptic church is the Christian church of Egypt and is closely associated with the Ethiopian Orthodox church.) But as he recounted this story to his children many times, he had looked his father's cows in the eye and said: "I don't care if the hyenas *do* eat you; I'm going away to make something of my life."

He found shelter at a French-speaking Catholic mission and was educated there until he reached his twenties. Then he was offered the chance to go to Paris for university training. Although he returned to Ethiopia to take up his life, the experience had a profound influence on him. He wanted all his children, girls as well as boys, to get the best education they could and to become whatever they wished. Instead of encouraging them to settle down and marry, he urged them to go abroad.

Says Almeza: "In our family my father broke the mold. He gave us this desire to better ourselves and our country. But then I had my older sisters as models, too. Both went to Paris for their university degrees."

Going abroad is the usual thing for Ethiopian students to do since there are only two institutions of higher learning in that country. "In 1982, 3,314 Ethiopian students were enrolled in institutions of higher learning abroad, more than were in schools of higher learning in the country itself. Of these, almost half went to the United States, with much smaller percentages going to Canada, West Germany, England, Cuba, and the countries of Eastern Europe." [10]

Since Almeza received her primary schooling in English rather than in French, her family sent her to the United States rather than to France to complete her education. In 1988 she was studying here for a master's degree in international studies.

Growing Up Peruvian

Feminism in modern Peru began in the early 1900s under the leadership of Maria Jesus Alvarado Rivera. A primary school dropout who later realized the importance of education, she spearheaded the suffrage movement in Peru and also protested the inequality of men and women under the law. But it was not until the 1960s that Peruvian peasant and educated women alike organized on a grand scale in order to affect social change. They wanted abortion on demand, readily available information on contraception, and changes in the constitution. They have not obtained all of their demands, but their voices continue to be heard. Lima, the nation's capital, has been a center of much of this political activity and in 1983 hosted the Second Feminist Conference of Latin America and the Caribbean.

It was in 1961, at the outset of Peru's feminist renaissance, that Eleana was born in the city of Lima. She was the second of four daughters, but she says neither of her parents ever seemed to mind having only girls. For the past twenty-five years, her mother has worked as a cashier in a department store. Until his death, her father was a policeman.

Like members of the various military divisions of the country such as the army and navy, the city's police and their families all live in one housing complex. Called "The Policeman's Village," it consists of roughly 600 homes as well as schools and shopping areas designated for the use of the resident police families.

Eleana recalls that in the mornings there would be an exodus of uniformed bodies streaming out of the homes in the complex. These included children on their way to the schools. Says Eleana: "School was very strict. Uniforms had to be kept clean, shoes shined. In high school we girls weren't permitted to wear make-up. . . . The teachers were mostly policemen themselves.

"Elementary school was co-ed; then at the high-school level boys and girls were separated. But the curriculum was much the same for both. And girls were encouraged to become active in sports."

In other ways, too, the lives of Eleana and her female classmates have been influenced by the recent change in ideas about women among Lima's middle class. A number of these young women have gone on to universities to study in fields ranging from accounting to physics.

4
GETTING AN EDUCATION

Girls and women in poor countries have been, and still are, the most disadvantaged group in the world with respect to education. Yet even within this group experiences with schooling vary depending upon family needs, wealth, traditions, and degree of Westernization.

The examples in this chapter reflect some of those factors. Despite the mixed report on the education of girls and women in the Third World, some developments inspire hope for the future.

The Middle East: Kuwait

Before 1950, the country of Kuwait—located between Saudi Arabia and Iraq—was a small, poor, technologically undeveloped sheikdom (a territory under the control of an Arab chief) of about 100,000 people.[1] Most of its adult male population eked out a living as fishermen, pearl divers, or animal herders. Other Kuwaiti men traveled long distances to trade their goods in the Arabian Gulf, India, and East Africa. A small minority—the sheiks and their kinsmen—formed the wealthy and noble elite of Kuwait society.

The women of this elite group remained veiled and secluded within the *harem,* or women's quarters. They did no housework, for this was done by poorer women hired for that purpose. The wives of ordinary men helped their husbands to support their families. In the *souk,* or marketplace, they sold vegetables, eggs, trinkets, and dresses, which they made by hand.

Then came the oil boom. Within twenty years, the number of people living in Kuwait increased more than sevenfold. Roughly half of the new population were immigrants lured there by the promise of economic opportunity. Oil transformed the little sheikdom into a modern city-state. Dwellings of mud and stone gave way to highrise apartments, shops, office buildings, all filled with the latest consumer items. What happened in the process to the veiled women of the *harem,* and to the hardworking wives and daughters of the fishermen, pearl divers, and merchants?

As early as 1965, nearly 67 percent of Kuwait's girls between five and nine years of age were attending government schools. There they constituted over 40 percent of the students in that age bracket. As you can see by comparing these figures with the statistics for a number of other developing countries in 1975 in Table 1, Kuwait was sending a larger proportion of its girls to school, in some cases more than twice the percentage, than other Middle East countries a decade later. In 1977, its adult female literacy rate was 50 percent, a rate also much higher than

Above: *the modern city of Kuwait.* Below: *some of the many Kuwaiti girls who regularly attend school, playing at recess. Kuwait is a leading Third World country in providing education to girls and women.*

Table 1
Statistics for School Attendance and Adult Literacy

	Percentage of Girls in School (1975)		Percentage of Boys in School (1975)		1977 Adult Literacy Rates (in percentage)	
	Age 6–11	Age 12–17	Age 6–11	Age 12–17	Female	Male
Libya	72	22	100	64	4	38
Egypt	52	27	80	49	29	57
Iran	50	40	81	67	26	69
Morocco	85	55	93	70	10	34
Pakistan	26	6	58	18	6	24
Saudi Arabia	24	20	46	32	1	5
Ghana	47	38	56	56	18	43
Kenya	91	40	98	58	10	30
Nigeria	32	14	45	24	6	25
Sudan	20	12	38	25	4	25
India	49	19	73	36	19	47
Indonesia	58	32	66	42	49	71
S. Korea	100	56	100	70	81	94
Thailand	76	29	80	39	70	87
Argentina	100	66	—	—	92	94
Chile	100	85	100	85	87	89
Colombia	67	56	—	—	80	82
Ecuador	79	52	79	56	70	78
Peru	78	67	81	80	62	83
Venezuela	74	58	53	75	73	80
Mexico	89	47	69	54	70	78
Guatemala	49	24	51	32	38	54
Nicaragua	57	48	54	47	47	58

Source: These statistics are found throughout the book *Sisterhood Is Global*, Robin Morgan, ed. (New York: Doubleday, Anchor Press, 1984).

in many Middle Eastern countries. Since 1966, education for six- to fourteen-year-olds has been free and compulsory in Kuwait.

Even before the construction of the University of Kuwait was completed in 1966, the government was encouraging young people to acquire university degrees. Scholarships were offered for Kuwaitis to study in colleges in Cairo, Alexandria, and Beirut. Some of these went to female students. In 1970, there were 246 women university graduates in the country. In almost all cases they were the first generation of their families to have this distinction. Upon their graduation, 99 percent went to work for their country's government. A quarter were hired as teaching assistants at the new University of Kuwait, and half of them got work as primary school teachers. (These are all government-paid positions.) This was in a year in which only 2.3 percent of the entire female population of Kuwait worked for wages.

Those first women graduates reported that they did experience inequality in their work life. They noted that, in general, men were promoted faster, were more likely to be given policy-making positions in government bureaus, and tended to downgrade the abilities of women on the job.

Nevertheless, the fact that a proportion of Kuwaiti women study and work side by side with men makes them unusual in the Muslim world. In neighboring Saudi Arabia, for example, "girls are educated in separate schools from the age of six. At [the] university, female students are completely segregated from the male students and the professors. They watch lectures on closed circuit television and ask questions by the telephones installed in the classrooms. They are given one day in the week to utilize the library, when male students are barred."[2] As a result of the recent revolution in Iran which brought fundamentalist Muslims to power, the government of that country has abolished sex-integrated schools. In some primary schools for girls, the students are also separated from their male teachers by a curtain.[3]

Whenever there is such rigid segregation by sex in education, there is the strong possibility of inequality. In Saudi Arabia, for example, in 1970 there were 395 schools for females as compared with 1,652 for males. And only 15 percent of its government's appropriations for educational and technical training in the years 1970 to 1975 were directed toward girls and women.[4]

Sexual segregation also tends to exclude girls and young women from certain activities and academic disciplines. The steering of students into particular careers according to their sex is a worldwide problem, but sexual segregation in schools makes the process of predetermining young people's career choices even easier. In Saudi Arabia, for example, women are not permitted to study engineering in any of the country's universities.[5] And in Iran, female students are effectively excluded from careers in science.[6] In Pakistan, co-ed schools are also being closed and according to a 1984 report there is in that country "a campaign to decrease or deny females admission to medical schools."[7]

Africa: Togo

In the suburbs of the African city of Lomé, the capital of Togo, girls attend secondary schools in almost equal proportion to boys. Here all courses, including sports, are co-ed. In 1978, Karen Biraimah, a graduate student at the State University of New York at Buffalo, decided to sit in on classes at one of the schools near Lomé to see if and how the experiences of girls and boys there differed.[8]

She spent time questioning the teachers about their expectations for these students, and she also spoke with the high school students themselves about their plans for the future. Finally, she examined the academic performances of the students. She wanted to see if the teachers' expectations were, in fact, borne out. The students came from a range of economic backgrounds.

The group targeted for study was at a level equivalent to the ninth grade in the American school system. Classes tended to be large; it wasn't unusual for a teacher to have ninety students in a room at one time. Roughly two-thirds of the teachers were men.

Ms. Biraimah distributed a questionnaire to the teachers asking them to describe their students from a list of thirty-seven terms. Table 2 shows their choices in order of the frequency with which the terms were used and for whom.

Table 2
Teacher-Selected Student Characteristics (Ranked)

Female Students	Male Students
1. Neat appearance	1. Likely to succeed at higher education
2. Below-average work	
3. Does not follow instruction	2. Good attendance
	3. Good in math
4. Lacks interest in school	4. Likely to obtain a good job after graduation
5. Does not profit from attending school	
	5. Responsible
6. Family well-educated	6. Aware of current events
7. Handles school property carefully	
	7. Hardworking
8. Quiet/submissive	8. Above-average work
9. Very emotional	9. Scholarly
10. Disruptive behavior	10. Leadership qualities

Source: Karen Coffyn Biraimah, "The Impact of Western Schools on Girls' Expectations: A Togolese Case," in *Women's Education in the Third World: Comparative Perspectives*, ed. Gail P. Kelly and Carolyn M. Elliott (Albany: The State University of New York Press, 1982), p. 192.

As you can see, the teachers tended to describe female students in terms of their appearance, males by the likelihood of their academic success. Teachers were much more negative about girls, at least in terms of their attendance, their character, and their potential for academic success.

To what extent do the teachers' perceptions correspond to reality? Not very much. The difference between the attendance records of girls and boys was rather small by the end of the year: 5 percent. And 32 percent of the girls, as compared with 39 percent of the boys, had passed their exams. The predicted difference in the two groups' success rates had been overestimated by their teachers.

Perhaps the teachers will also be wrong in their predictions about their female students' futures. For the most part they foresaw these girls employed in low-status, low-paying jobs, or else in nurturing professions. In terms of the frequency of response, these were listed as nurse, office worker, housewife, hairdresser, seamstress, primary school teacher, midwife.

The girls themselves presented quite a different picture. Not one of them mentioned wanting to be a housewife as a sole occupation. And 80 percent of those questioned expected to go to a university. When asked why they wanted to go, the majority said that it was necessary for having a real career. And they know the names of important women in Togolese history and society. Apparently it is those women, not the teachers, who provide the real motivation for these girls.

Were there any differences in the classroom performances of these African girls and boys? Watching the interaction between teachers and students over a period of months, Ms. Biraimah noted that the girls volunteered answers a good deal less frequently than the boys, but that when they did answer, their responses were equal to those of the boys.

She notes, too, that "although the female students generally played a marginal academic role in the classroom,

*School girls in Morocco proudly hold up
their answers in a math class.*

they were not forgotten when 'housekeeping' duties were
assigned. Not only did the girls do all the sweeping before
class . . . they were also called upon three times as often
as their male counterparts to do in-class maintenance tasks
such as cleaning the boards or returning papers."[9] This
reminds us that getting an education involves more than
learning the subject matter being taught. From an early
age we are constantly being taught what is expected of
us, and also what *isn't* expected of us, by those in author-
ity. To their credit, the Togolese girls do not, at least at
the moment, seem to be absorbing the lesson being offered them concerning female inferiority. But this is a difficult matter to assess. How can we measure the effect of
making girls responsible for classroom "housekeeping"?

India

. . . The fact that psychological differences between the two sexes arise not out of sex, but out of social conditioning, will have to be widely publicized, and people will have to be made to realize that stereotypes of "masculine" and "feminine" personalities do more harm than good.[10]

These words are from the government of India's 1965 proposal to create a school curriculum that would promote equality of the sexes. A direct result of the proposal was the government's assessment of textbooks used at various levels of schooling throughout the nation and a commitment to make Indian schoolbooks nonsexist. To make sure this goal was reached, the government established guidelines in textbook writing.

Fifteen years later, a study was made of forty-one textbooks then in use.[11] Twenty of these were written in Hindi, the national language, and twenty-one were in English, also an important language in instruction in India. Each of the books had an annual readership of more than a million secondary school students in a number of different Indian states. What did the books teach about the natures of men and women? One thing they taught was that men are more visible in society, since one major finding of the study was that in these books male characters predominate; in 75 percent of the lessons they were the leading figures. And there were seven times as many biographical portraits of men as of women.

Perhaps even more signifiant was the way the books portrayed men and women. Females were most often de-

Children with their teacher during recess at a co-ed Indian elementary school

scribed by their physical appearance and were cited for their obedience and self-sacrifice. They were also depicted as weak, vain, and irrational. Men, on the other hand, were shown to be brave, intelligent, adventurous, innovative movers.

The books mentioned a total of 463 occupations; 363 of them were mentioned in conjunction with male characters only. Of the twelve occupations assigned only to female characters, most were either low in prestige or required semiskilled labor. They included: cleaning woman, nun, prostitute, and housewife. The highest number of female characters in the textbooks appear in the role of housewife.

In some of the lessons, the message is more direct. One text published in 1976 states: "There are certain things in this world that are meant for the males and higher education is one such thing . . . if the females, too . . . begin to read English newspapers and discuss politics then what would happen to the domestic chores!"[12]

A lesson called "Choosing A Career" reads as follows: "A boy may have an aptitude for engineering. . . . Both boys and girls can become laboratory technicians and girls can take up nursing."[13] The possibility of girls having an aptitude for engineering or boys for nursing is not raised here.

These lessons within lessons seem contrary to the stated goal of the Indian government: to make people realize that male and female personalities are not fixed at birth, but that they are stereotypes created largely by what we are *taught* to expect of men and women.

Latin America

Look again at the figures for school attendance and adult literacy around the Third World (Table 1). You will find that the rates for Latin American countries are, in general, much higher than elsewhere for both men and women.

Between 1950 and 1970, literacy more than doubled in some of these countries.

Compared with women in Africa and the Middle East, those of Latin America have had a relatively long history of participation in higher education. In Chile, for example, women were permitted to enter universities by presidential decree back in 1877. (In comparison, that right was first established for Saudi women almost a century later.) Ten years after the 1877 decree, the first Chilean women received doctorates in medicine, a field which is more accessible to women in some Latin American countries than it is to North American women.

At the lower levels, what is the effect, if any, of education on Latin American women's ability to become wage earners? To answer this question, Catalina Wainerman analyzed the 1970 education and labor statistics for women in two rather different Latin American countries: Argentina and Paraguay.[14] Argentina is highly urban, industrial, and literate. Paraguay is a more rural, agricultural country with lower literacy rates and higher fertility rates.

Despite the differences, Ms. Wainerman found that the women of the two countries worked for wages to a similar degree. They represented between a fifth and a quarter of their respective nations' wage earners. The difference lay in the kinds of jobs they held. Although a large number of Argentine women worked as domestic help, many also were employed in the professions. In Paraguay more women worked on the land and in agriculture-related jobs. Proportionately twice as many Argentine women (40 percent) completed primary school as women the same age in Paraguay.

What remains the same in each country is this: the higher the level of education attained by the women of any age group, the better the chances are that those women work for wages.[15] In both countries, and elsewhere in Latin America, schooling is more critical for women seeking jobs than it is for men. In Chile, for example, a woman who

A co-ed classroom in Honduras. In Central and South America, girls, as well as boys, have been encouraged to read and learn.

drops out of secondary school has about the same chance of getting a semiskilled job as a man who did not complete primary school.[16]

In Paraguay, education also seems to be related to the production of babies. Here, as almost everywhere, people who attend a university tend to marry and begin having families later in life. But the relationship between education and fertility is not limited to the college educated. In Paraguay, illiterate women over forty years of age were found to have an average of twice as many children as those who had secondary level education. This is a pattern found in many, but not all, developing countries.

From Hopelessness Come
the Seeds of Hope

The study of the educational opportunities and experiences of women in the Third World is in its infancy and there is still much to be learned. A lot of what we now know comes from research spurred by the U.N. Decade For Women. This research indicates that sexual segregation—with its unequal allotment of funds for women's facilities, Victorian stereotypes found in textbooks and classroom teaching, different courses of study for girls and boys, and the steering of girls into a small range of jobs that are low in pay and prestige—has characterized female education in recent years throughout much of the world.

One other obstacle to female education should also be mentioned. Girls in all developing countries who live in rural areas have the worst chances of any sector of the world's population to get even a primary school education. In cities, girls generally have fewer chances than boys to attend secondary school and university. A higher proportion of girls than boys drop out at all levels in countries as different as Mexico, Ghana, Kenya, and Pakistan.[17] Why is this so? A major reason is that parents are more likely to withdraw their daughters than their sons from school when children's services are needed at home.

As a result, opening more schools, even co-ed schools, in Third World countries is not always enough to ensure that girls will attend them. As long as girls are expected, from an early age, to engage in such vitally important domestic labor as gathering water and fuel, their families won't encourage them to go to school. It's as important for governments wishing to promote equal education to dig wells in rural areas as it is to build schools.

Despite the current inequalities, there are developments to inspire hope for the future. For example:

- In 1979 the Moroccan government began a training program that allowed women to study electronics and industrial architecture and design—fields that represented completely new opportunities for the women of that country.

- The International Metalworkers Federation and the International Labor Organization have initiated a project aimed at teaching marketable skills to women in Nicaragua.

- In the Philippines, women have, since 1950, achieved equality with men at all levels of education and constitute nearly half of the college faculties in that country.

- In Africa the illiteracy rate for women has dropped from 82 percent in 1970 to 73 percent in 1980.

- The government of Tunisia has consciously attempted to offer equal educational opportunities to both sexes with the result that female school attendance in Tunisia has increased significantly.

5

MARRIAGE AND MOTHERHOOD

In most countries of the world—whether developed or developing nations—getting married, being a wife, and raising a family are still viewed by most people as the goals all women should have. We may think we Americans are different but, in fact, in this country millions of men and women of all religions, ethnic backgrounds, and social positions still believe women should find fulfillment in marriage and children. In addition, millions of American women want to get married and bear children, even if they also want to work, make money, or travel.

Some of the customs surrounding marriage and child-raising found in Third World countries are quite similar to those found in the West. Others, such as arranged marriages and polygamy, are quite different. In India the steps leading to marriage are highly developed and ritualized. In the Islamic Middle East, a young woman's lack of freedom to choose a mate is colored further by the various religious and secular laws that sometimes keep her a prisoner in her house or tent. Non-Muslims and Muslim African women have to contend further with their husbands having other wives.

Becoming a mother changes a woman's status in all countries, and Third World nations are no exception. Usually a mother is treated better than a woman yet to bear children. Women who bear no children are still pitied or scorned as they have been in most countries historically. While only a few examples are given in this chapter, they typify the experiences of millions of women in Third World countries.

Marriage and Motherhood
in India

In 1978, Madulika was nineteen years old and living at home with her family in a rural village in central India. Being good Hindu parents, her mother and father were concerned that a proper husband be found for her. So, as Hindu parents have been doing since ancient times, they set out, with the aid of their relatives and friends, to find Mr. Right and to arrange the marriage.

Nowadays in developing countries like India, many university-educated young men leave to find work in Europe or North America. As a result, these young men, who are viewed as highly desirable matches, cannot always be viewed in person by parents seeking a mate for their daughters. But this is not considered to be a major problem. It is neither the boy's looks, the sound of his voice, nor his personality that concern them. It is his other credentials they are interested in. These have to do mainly with his financial position and his family background.

In making their original selections, Madulika's parents and their investigative helpers made sure that all the boys came from "good" families. By this they meant that all the families were of the Hindu religion, originally from their own home region, of roughly the same economic background as themselves, and of their own "community." In India this term refers to named, ranked hereditary groups. Formerly, birth into a particular community determined a person's occupation and social standing in the town or village. Today that is less true, but community membership does put limits on eligible marriage partners, at least in those cases where parents do the arranging.

After Madulika's parents had investigated, visited, and negotiated with several families having eligible sons, they narrowed their choice down to three. Then they presented their daughter with the names and addresses of the three young men. As it turned out, all three worked abroad. On the basis of her correspondence with them, Madulika would have to decide which one to marry. She wrote to all three men—a lab technician in London, a diplomat serving in Canada, and an electrical engineer living in Rochester, New York. Soon she had three photographs and three small bundles of mail to pore over. Still she couldn't decide among them.

Within six months, two of the suitors—the men working in London and Canada—found reason to return briefly to India. On separate occasions each made his way to the village where Madulika lived to pay her a visit. During these visits Madulika and her suitor were always strictly chaperoned by her relatives. They were never completely alone. After the second visitor left, Madulika's parents pressed her for an answer. They would stand for no more shilly-shallying on her part.

"I will marry the man in Rochester," she announced. Her parents then made it clear that her decision must be final. They planned to inform the man's family and go forward with the wedding arrangements immediately. Madulika assented. When asked why she had chosen the one man of the three she hadn't ever seen, she replied that it would be more romantic that way. And so it was that two months later she caught her first glimpse of her husband—during their wedding ceremony. She herself was so thoroughly veiled that all he could clearly see of her was her eyes. Days later, Madulika left everything and everyone she knew behind and followed this man to a new life half-way around the world.

Although it sounds extraordinary to us, Madulika's experience is typical of the marriages of today's middle-class Indian women. In some respects it also typifies Indian marriage arrangements generally. In all groups, for example, it is quite normal for the family to either select the groom or narrow down the possibilities to two or three men. Only in the most Westernized circles, accounting for less than 1 percent of the country's population, do young people date and freely choose their own mates.[1] Formerly husband- and wife-to-be met only briefly, if at all, before the wedding. One contributing factor was that customary Hindu marriage rules required husbands and wives to come from different, often distant, villages or from different neighborhoods of the same city.

Love and romance are not entirely missing from this system, but they are thought about rather differently. Romance in India has less to do with the wooing of a particular love object than with the mystery surrounding an imagined life with an as-yet-unknown person. Love is not something marriages are expected to start out with. In fact, the daytime—or rather, public—relations between husband and wife tend to be quite formal, at least in the early years of marriage. But love between spouses is expected to grow, though it is often not until middle and old age that husband and wife can publicly relax in each other's company.

In any case, the marriage contract is normally for life. Before 1949, divorce in Hindu India did not exist. Though now a legal possibility, it is still very rare. Even in educated circles it is usually unthinkable because of the great shame that people attach to it.

An Indian bride and groom sit amid flowers during their wedding ceremony. Sometimes it is at their wedding that the bride and groom meet for the first time.

Madulika's use of the mail to "meet" unknown potential fiancés is also not unusual. Some urban families even use newspaper ads for tracking down suitable mates for their offspring. Indian immigrant newspapers in the United States and Great Britain bring a transatlantic dimension to the process. Here, for example, is a typical ad listed in the matrimonial page of *India Abroad*, published weekly in New York City:

> Correspondence invited from North Indian Rajput [the name of a community] professional man for a bright, beautiful woman, 24 years old, 5'2"; pleasant-natured, home-loving, cultured. Please reply with details and photograph.

You might imagine from the ad that it was placed by an Indian woman seeking an alternative to the arranged marriage system. You would probably be wrong. In all likelihood the young woman is in India and the ad was placed by a brother working in the United States. He will receive the initial replies and photos. He will screen the applicants and send the names of the ones he deems suitable for his sister back to the family in India. They will continue the investigation of the applicants from their side. Only when the family has concluded its inquiries and negotiations will the addresses of the final choices be given to the girl. Then the correspondence will begin!

Traditionally the pre-wedding negotiations involved discussion of the dowry, the financial assistance the bride's family gives the couple upon their marriage. This used to take the form of land and basic household furnishings. In today's commercial economy the dowry more frequently consists of a sum of cash. In urban, middle-class families it is often supplemented by electronic equipment such as stereos and television sets, and other modern consumer items. In 1961, demanding a dowry was technically made illegal, but the law was so vague and ill-enforced that it might as well never have been drawn at all. Most families with daughters expect to make the huge outlay.

The groom's *background* is scrutinized by the girl's family to ensure that the boy will be a faithful husband and good provider. The potential bride *herself* is scrutinized by the boy's family. The traditional setting for the first interview is the girl's home.

The boy's family may or may not allow him to attend, but in any case a number of his male relatives—brothers, or cousins, perhaps—will go along to observe and report back to him as to the appearance and demeanor of his chosen bride. The main inquisitor is the boy's father. Except for the girl being interviewed, women are frequently excluded from the proceedings. The candidate, dressed to look her very best, serves the men snacks and may entertain them with a song or performance on a musical instrument. She also answers their questions: Can she prepare such and such a dish? Does she know a particular ritual? Has she read a specific book?

The men are interested less in her replies than her manner of reply. Even upper-class, college-educated young women are subjected to this anxiety-producing interview. In such a case Manisha Roy says that the men note "if she has been spoiled by Western college education or if she is still very quiet, subdued, and docile. It is important for her to show signs of obedience and docility if she is to make a good wife and daughter-in-law." [2] Ideally she should speak in short sentences and keep her eyes cast downward when addressing any of the males present.

Urban, less traditional families may at some point arrange for a joint trip to a restaurant so that the bride- and groom-to-be can observe each other at least once before their wedding while still under the watchful eyes of adults of both families. It may be a month or more before they see each other again, most likely at the wedding. Speaking of the moment when her parents announced the completion of her marriage negotiations, a young Calcutta woman told Dr. Roy: "I felt a sharp tinge of happiness, then tried to remember the face of the man who had offered a cup of tea to me in the restaurant." [3]

Though this young woman's plight may seem unusual to Westerners, it is not atypical in India where even today the majority of marriages are arranged by the families of the bride and groom. What follows the selection of the mate and the courtship, however, is far more familiar to us.

First there is a whirlwind shopping spree. The future bride accompanies her mother and aunts as they purchase a new wardrobe for the girl and the household furnishings that will form a part of her dowry. The remainder of the dowry will be in cash, but that will be given along with the girl herself by her father at the marriage ceremony.

Regardless of whether the family is from the city or the countryside, the wedding festivities will take place over a three-day period. Hundreds of friends and relatives are likely to be invited. This wedding is a big event. It is one the bride has been steered toward all her life, like a satellite en route to its mother ship in a distant corner of the galaxy. Yet strangely, when the celebrating is finally over, it may seem to her that she is something less than she was before. Why is this so?

During the months, and to some degree even the years, before her wedding, the Indian girl is treated somewhat like a guest in her own home. She is indulged by all the household members but most especially by her mother. It isn't only because the mother knows that she will soon lose her daughter to another family; she also knows that the initial phase of marriage may bring loneliness and disappointment as well.

If the bride is a rural village girl, her loneliness is apt to be all the greater, for after the wedding she typically moves to the distant household of her new husband and his family. There she discovers that in marrying she has not so much gained a husband as a mother-in-law. In India, as in some other countries, being a good wife means being a good daughter-in-law.

In the village setting, being a good daughter-in-law isn't

easy, at least at first. When the new bride first settles in at her husband's household, she finds herself in the lowest position there. It's more than being "the new kid on the block." Tradition requires that she absolutely avoid direct communication with any of the village men who aren't relatives. What is more, she must avoid contact of any sort with her husband's older brothers, even those living in the very same house. Fortunately, she may speak, and even joke, with any of her husband's younger brothers.

Though she addresses her new sisters-in-law as "sister," this often simply reminds her how much she misses her real sisters back home where she was treated like a comparative princess. Here in her husband's home she is expected to do the hardest and biggest share of the household chores. Like Cinderella, she awakes at dawn to begin work that continues late into the night. And always, she is the last one to eat.

Her husband remains in many ways a stranger to her. They cannot be daytime companions according to the etiquette of Indian village life. Public displays of affection between husband and wife, even newlyweds, are highly discouraged. Husbands and wives are not even supposed to praise each other in the presence of others. In fact, they do not even utter each other's first names except when alone together. To do otherwise would be considered bad form, behavior that's not quite acceptable. The outward relationship between husband and wife has therefore been engineered into one of great cordiality. And at night in crowded households young spouses may not have all that much privacy.

Small wonder then that a young husband appears in the eyes of his new wife to be far closer with his mother than with herself. The pattern is borne out by a survey done in one rural Indian community. According to sociologist Madhav S. Gore, 56 percent of the married men questioned said they felt closer to their mothers than to their wives; only 20 percent said they felt closer to their wives.[4]

The lowly status of a young Indian rural wife in her new household changes drastically the day she announces she is to have a baby. Suddenly, instead of being seen as just a workhorse, she is someone of great importance. Everyone, including the household women, become very concerned with her welfare. They see that she eats well, rests often, does not exert herself by doing too much work. Her new family's affection and pride in her increase as the child grows inside her.[5] According to Indian psychologist Sudhir Kakar, even her husband now respects her because she has become a "proper" woman. In India, as in most other places, becoming a mother is considered the "attainment of the status a woman is born to achieve."[6] Women who do not become pregnant within two to five years after their marriage are made to feel that they are most unfortunate. Village women who appear to be barren submit themselves to long and physically painful ceremonial rituals aimed at making them fertile.[7]

In such circumstances it is not surprising that the use of contraceptives, both modern and traditional, is minimal. Modern contraceptives are not readily available and even where they are village women do not always know how to use them correctly. Some distrust contraceptives simply because the government encourages their use and villagers distrust the government on principle.[8] But apart from these problems, there is the inescapable fact that for a village woman the only way to affirm—and to keep on reaffirming—her identity is by becoming a mother.

Perhaps it is because her relationship to her young husband is generally so formal that the Indian woman's ties

Mothers with their children wait patiently for a meal at the Nutrition Rehabilitation Center in southern India.

to her children are so binding. While they are infants, her involvement with them is very great, to the near exclusion even of her husband. Shortly after the birth she might well leave him to return to her parents—with the baby, of course—for a visit lasting several months.

While having children is smiled upon, having them in too rapid succession is not. Couples are therefore expected to avoid sexual relations not only during the pregnancy, but for two years after the birth of their baby. During this period the child usually sleeps next to the mother at night. In rural areas children are breast-fed on demand until the age of two or three years, even though they are also getting additional foods by this time.

The care of Indian children falls almost entirely to their mothers and to a lesser extent to the other adult females in the household. In any case it is the mother's attention that a child most loudly calls for, and it seems that Indian mothers are extremely patient in meeting their demands. Their slogan seems to be: "The child is always right!" These mothers are not dismayed if their children do not keep to a schedule of any sort. They do not push children into achieving particular skills. Rather they allow them to develop at their own pace. They do not discipline or punish them if they act unsocially. Such skills, it is assumed, will come in their own good time. For now they can do no wrong because they are just little children.

Sudhir Kakar argues that what makes Indian mothers so indulgent is their gratitude toward their infants. They bring their mothers such great public esteem, both within the family circle and Indian society at large, just by the very fact of their existence![9]

Arranged marriages are the norm in other countries besides India. But in some countries of the Third World, women also have to contend with polygyny, the practice of a man's taking more than one wife simultaneously. Here the road to equality is long and rough. Women are still fighting for equal rights in marriage in Western countries like the United States and Great Britain. But imagine their plight in developing countries where tradition and financial conditions often combine to make it difficult for them not only to choose their husband, should they wish to marry, but also to opt for remaining single if that is their wish.

Marriage, Polygyny, and Divorce
in the Muslim Middle East

Men's souls are naturally inclined to covetousness. But if ye be kind towards women, and fear to wrong them, God is well acquainted with what ye do.

—The Koran

These words are from the Koran, the Muslim book of holy scriptures. Written in Arabic in the seventh century A.D., this book also became the source of traditional law in the Islamic countries of the world. Mohammed, the author of the Koran, wished to improve the lot of Arab women. Until then they had no legal status at all; they were given in marriage without their consent, they had no property rights to speak of, and only a husband could terminate a marriage at will.

Unfortunately for Arab women, Mohammed did not provide specific rules for instituting changes. Instead he called on men to "respect women" and to "give them what is due them" (referring to their inheritance). In the generations that followed, these strictures were interpreted in the light of the old ways. Not until our own century, and in some places only in its third quarter, has the higher education of some Muslim women brought about pressure for reforming the laws affecting family life. Referred to collectively as the Personal Status Laws, these concern marriage, divorce, and child custody.

All divisions of Islam, the predominant religion of the Middle East and North Africa, recognize the rights of a "marriage guardian."[10] This person, usually a girl's father or one of his male relatives, is responsible for contracting the marriage. Traditionally this was done at the time of a baby's birth, although the marriage would not be celebrated or consummated until many years later. The religious law did not require the consent of the bride unless the marriage guardian had been someone other than her father or her paternal grandfather. Today the secular laws of most Muslim countries make marriage without the consent of the bride illegal. But there are ways that a family can pressure a girl into going through with a marriage she doesn't really want.

The Koranic law allowed a man to have up to four wives at a time. Furthermore, he didn't need the permission of any of his wives to take on another. The Koran says that a man shouldn't marry additional wives unless he can treat them all equally. Recently Muslim feminists have argued that it is impossible for anyone to treat four people equally in every respect. They say Mohammed knew this and included this sentence in order to eliminate polygyny. But traditionally the statement was interpreted to refer to a man's capacity to provide equal support for his wives. In any case, the Koran left the judgment—of whether or not he could treat his wives equally—up to the man himself.

Polygyny has been made illegal in Tunisia, Turkey, and the Muslim states of the Soviet Union. Other Islamic countries have sought to make the wife's permission necessary. In 1978, Syria required a husband to prove to a court that he was capable of supporting additional wives, but permission of his first wife wasn't necessary. In the same year Pakistan required only that a polygynous marriage be approved by a local council.

In 1970, the actual practice of polygyny in the Muslim areas that permitted it was about 10 percent of all marriages contracted in those countries.[11] But the fact that it exists as a possibility can have a real effect on a woman's social and reproductive behavior. She knows that if she displeases her husband, another wife may appear on the scene. The same may happen if she does not produce sons soon after her marriage.

Under traditional Muslim law a wife could not obtain a divorce no matter how badly her husband treated her. On the other hand, a man could divorce his wife without having to give any reason. The procedure was simple. All the husband had to do was to pronounce *talaq*. Translated, this essentially means, "I hereby divorce you" (literally, "I repudiate you"). After three months had passed the divorce was official. If the husband said *talaq* three times in succession, the divorce took effect immediately.

Reforms regarding this custom did not begin until the 1920s in Lebanon, Egypt, and the Sudan. A decade later India and Pakistan gave Muslim women the right to divorce their husbands on specific grounds. In most Islamic countries it wasn't until the 1960s and later that men were no longer allowed to divorce their wives at will outside a court of law. Today most Muslim countries require men to show good cause for divorce. A 1975 law in Iran placed men and women on an equal basis in the matter of obtaining a divorce, but this law was repealed by the revolutionary government in 1979.

Some Muslim countries now require men to pay their divorced wives money toward their support for a short period, sometimes up to a year. Long-term alimony payments are not expected because it is assumed that a divorced woman will remarry quickly. Normally she returns to her own family and a search is immediately begun for a new partner. If unsuccessful, she may be expected to seek salaried employment in order to support herself.

Child support is not usually paid by the husband because both the old Koranic law and the new secular laws generally give custody of children to the mother for only a brief time. Formerly, children who had reached the age

of seven were returned to their fathers, or to someone related to the father through the male line. Regardless of the age or sex of the children, the mother ordinarily lost custody of them when she remarried.

Today the laws of most Muslim countries grant a court the right to decide who obtains custody of the children and these laws make the welfare of the child all-important. However, some experts feel that there is still often "a presumption that the welfare of the child is best served by applying the strict rules of the traditional law . . ."[12]

The law can be very fickle indeed. In Egypt, for example, in the 1970s, despite opposition from Muslim conservatives, President Anwar Sadat decreed that a man must officially notify his wife if he planned to take a second; that this second marriage could be used as grounds for divorce by the first wife if she refused to permit it and the man did not heed her; and that in such cases custody of the children went to the wife. But in 1985, the Supreme Court of Egypt repealed these new laws. Similarly, Iran's laws changed when the fundamentalist and revolutionary government came to power in 1979.

Getting Married in Ghana, West Africa

Everywhere the history of marriage is as firmly embedded in economics as a pearl is in an oyster. In the West African country of Ghana the relationship between marriage and the economic system is particularly clear. Here in the past century both institutions have changed radically and

A Muslim woman and her child.
In Muslim society, as in much of
the Third World, it is important
that women have sons.

in ways that help us to see how closely the two are connected.

Originally the indigenous population, known as the Ga, were an agricultural people. Before the era of colonialism, their system of marriage was, among other things, a way of continuing the corporate life of a *patrilineage*. This was the kin group that owned a particular parcel of land in common. It consisted of those men, women, and children who were related to one another through male links.

Polygyny was another feature of traditional Ga marriage. Westerners tend to take a negative view of this practice. In *The Chief*, a novel that takes place in a West African country, the character Tunde gives some of the practical reasons behind this practice in the past:

> "First a farmer acquired wives to help him raise his crops. Then, second, it was a means of timing births, since a woman does not have relations with her husband for at least one and a half years after the birth of a child—usually longer. Third, and most crucial reason, some women do not have children, And other children died, in former times as well as now, and so another wife was taken to have children replace those who had died."
>
> "Do you think this custom will continue?"
>
> "I doubt for long as it is too expensive to support two families today."[13]

As in many parts of the world, Ga girls or young women would upon marriage move from their own family's land to the patrilineage of the husband. Here the new wife would live and work among her husband's parents, siblings, other wives, their offspring, and the wives and offspring of the husband's brothers and male cousins. As in India, marriage entailed elaborate negotiations and was usually for life.

The negotiations began when a man sent a small sum of money and a special drink to the girl's parents. If they accepted these, negotiations could proceed further. Before the couple were pronounced man and wife, a series of five or six different payments, which traditionally took the form of bolts of cloth, would be made to the girl's parents. The term for this transaction translates as "giving cloth to replace that which the girl dirtied as a child." The idea behind the gifts was to compensate the parents for the expense of raising their daughter, whose labor they were about to lose. A third series of gifts to the bride's parents climaxed with the marriage itself when the bride, decked out in a completely new outfit, was paraded around the town or village on the shoulders of her female relatives. Those men who were too poor to provide the large number of gifts could instead work for the bride's father on her family's land for an agreed-upon period of time.

Today these patrilineages or kin groups no longer own or control land. The colonial governments in Africa often required that corporately owned lineage lands be officially deeded to particular individuals, specifically male individuals. Consequently, today land tends to be owned by a relatively small number of men rather than being held in common by related men and women with equal access to its use. In the process, the lineages lost much of their political power. They also lost the power to arrange the marriages of their young people.

A 1978 survey of one hundred Ga women between the ages of thirty-nine and fifty living in the city of Accra in Ghana showed that fewer than one-third of them had had arranged marriages.[14] Even the traditional series of gifts to the bride's parents have all but been dispensed with. Now a woman's fiancé simply "offers a drink" to them in memory of the old wedding custom. Then the engagement is considered official.

According to the women interviewed, the obligations of a Ga husband were: to provide food, clothing, and medical aid for his wife and his children and to pay for the education of the children. Among the obligations of a wife were: fidelity, showing submission to the husband in most matters, doing all the cooking, doing the laundry (washing machines are rare here), and caring for the children. Cooking is considered especially important by Ga men and women. When a wife refuses to cook for her husband it is supposed that she is giving a sign that a serious quarrel is in progress—it might even forewarn a separation. Another obligation wives accepted was that of selling in the marketplace in order to earn money for household expenses.

The same study of Accra women showed that about 40 percent of them were partners in polygynous marriages.[15] Ga women object to polygyny for reasons that might surprise a Westerner. They say that it is not the loss of their husband's time or affection that irritates them, but rather the fact that limited resources must be spread even more thinly. Each new wife represents a further drain on a husband's resources. Women especially fear the resulting competition among the children for their father's inheritance. But if a husband really could manage to fulfill his economic obligations to each of his wives and children, then in general the women were not hostile to the idea of sharing him.

Still, most marriages in Accra are not polygynous. Ghanaian men who have received some higher education are apt to be married to a single wife at one time, as are many less educated men who cannot "afford" more than one wife. Educated wives often exert pressure to also have their marriage registered. This means marrying in a church or registry office—something that is frequently done months, or even years, after the marriage has taken place according to traditional custom. Marriages that are registered can be dissolved only by divorce procedures taken in the High Court. They also give more security to wives than do marriages contracted only under customary law. In the case of an officially granted divorce, a wife has the right to claim support benefits from her ex-husband. Divorce was also possible in the days when the patrilineages were powerful, but there was an elaborate and formal procedure involved. Today in the case of marriages contracted under customary law and which are dissolved, neither partner receives financial support from the other.

A 1974 study of eighty-three men who worked in Accra as civil servants showed that more than two-thirds of their wives had finished secondary school, with a small minority having some university training.[16] The majority of these wives work full time as primary school teachers, nurses, or clerks. A few worked part time as seamstresses or vendors. The households of these couples ranged in size from half a dozen to fifteen individuals. These people included not only children, but also either paid domestic help or distant relatives serving as live-in help, as well as siblings and nieces and nephews of the husband and wife.

Some well-educated, urban Ghanaian couples, like poorer, rural couples, must be separated for long periods of time. This is partly because the process of obtaining a university degree can take a long time if one has to work at the same time. Most Ghanaian men do not have the luxury of going to school full time, and most couples marry before they have been graduated. Then, too, those in civil service posts are frequently required to travel to distant locations both inside and outside the country. The demands of such a life-style are illustrated by the case of the Ansahs, a Ghanaian couple who calculate that they have spent most of their eight years of married life apart.

> Mr. Ansah met and courted his wife when he was a junior civil servant and just about to go to university. . . . They met and married in their home town first according to customary rites, and then at the insistence of the wife's father, in church. . . .
>
> Within a couple of months Mr. Ansah left for university and his wife worked as a midwife in her home town until her first child was born at her parents' home. As soon as the baby was three months old she went to work at a hospital 50 miles away. Her cousin stayed with her for a year to take care of the baby. Each month her husband travelled by lorry [truck] from the university to visit her.

A month before her second baby was due, Mr. Ansah's wife stopped work and went to stay with her parents. . . . The following year she got a transfer to her home town. . . . Her third child was delivered in her maternal grandmother's house. By then her husband finished his course, got a job in Accra, and rented accommodations. She went there to join him, taking her own brother to attend school there as well as a maid and her three small children. The husband already had two of his sons by his first marriage staying with him to attend school and his sister's son. By the following year the Ansahs were also accommodating the wife's sister and the husband's third child by his first marriage.[17]

Being a Wife and Mother
in West Africa

In West African, as in rural Indian, households, husbands and wives do not generally regard each other as companions. Historian Claire Robertson goes so far as to say that today in Ghana, a Ga woman's most important emotional ties "are usually with her mother and children; her siblings rank next in importance; her husband a poor third."[18]

It used to be that men in most West African societies were supposed to provide for their wives and children. But changes in the economy have made women more and more responsible for supporting themselves and their children. The trend began with the large-scale migration of African men during the first half of this century. In search of work, millions left their small farms in the interior for the mining towns within their country's borders or the coastal cities farther still. Here in most cases wage labor was available exclusively to men. Some colonial governments went so far as to pass laws prohibiting women to come to the cities. The men's wives remained home on the family land and with only the help of children managed to wrest a living from it. They grew food crops to feed their families and sold the surplus in local markets. At best, husbands commuted between farm and town. But many were gone for years at a time.

Even today when women are permitted to migrate to the cities of Africa and when the ratio between urban men and women has begun to equalize, the problems are far from over. Political and economic forces still separate many families. In black South Africa, for example, "it is not uncommon for a married couple to spend most of their lives apart."[19] And in Accra, Ghana, the 1978 survey referred to earlier showed that fewer than half of the women in the sample lived in the same city as their husbands.

With husbands living far away, women often find themselves having to provide a larger share of their children's support. In addition, many of these women also support their aging parents. It is a large burden. In 1970, almost half of Accra's population was either under fifteen or over sixty-five.[20] It is the city's young women—daughters, nieces, and granddaughters—who do the cooking and tending of older female relatives. Elderly men are also cared for by women—their youngest wife.

In Africa, city women manage to support all these people on the earnings of their market activities—the trading of foodstuffs and dry goods. They are therefore self-employed, and when they themselves get too old to work they receive no social security benefits. Who provides for them then? Their children, and in particular their daughters. As a result, poorer African women see in children not only the satisfaction of emotional needs, but also a form of social security. This may well be their main reason for having so many babies. The 1978 survey showed that the Ga women of Accra have an average of six children. It seems they also have the habit of hoping that one of them will succeed in a big way, or that at least one will not move far away and forget their aging mother. Investing in lots of children is the only way these women have of planning for a retirement.

As we can see from the examples offered in this chapter, the concerns and problems of married women vary depending upon the country as well as the economic background of the individual. In some groups, wives are denied the right to work; in others they struggle alone to support themselves and their children. In some countries divorced women are denied custody of their children; in others they must engage in legal battles to obtain help from their former husbands in supporting their children. Everywhere the experiences of marriage and motherhood are colored by economic considerations as well as by the local customs surrounding these changes in status.

ON THE LAND

Jill Kasdan arose at 6:00 A.M. As usual, she fixed breakfast for her husband and herself, tidied the kitchen, dressed, then traveled an hour by public transportation to a distant corner of New York City to attend an eight o'clock class at a municipal college. After the two-hour class, she went to the library where she checked out the half dozen books she would need to consult in the following days for her doctoral research. Then she hauled them home with her. They weighed more than thirty pounds.

Back at her apartment, Jill changed into jeans and downed a sandwich. Then she went to the laundromat several blocks away to put in a load of wash, stopping on her return to do the day's grocery shopping. After putting the groceries away, she swept the floors, vacuumed, and cleaned the bathroom. Then she traipsed back to the laundromat to put the wash in the dryer.

Home again, she began cooking dinner. Then she did some bookkeeping for her husband's business and finally began to read for her own research. Soon, though, she was back at the laundromat to gather the finished wash. In the elevator on her return to the apartment, a retired male neighbor greeted her: "So you're not one of the working girls, I see!"

Ms. Kasdan reports that upon hearing this she had to stifle an impulse to strangle her neighbor with her husband's newly laundered longjohns. But later the remark made her think. It was midafternoon and she was at home. She was not crisply dressed or carefully coiffed, nor was she armed with a briefcase. She did not receive cash for what she did. Therefore, no matter how many calories she expended or tasks she accomplished in a given day, she would not be perceived by her neighbor, nor indeed by the U.S. Labor Department, as "working."

In Third World countries, particularly in the agricultural regions, the situation is much the same but with dire consequences. There women work hard to feed their families and their nations. But for the most part their labor is not officially recognized; at the very best, it is underreported. As a result, many well-meaning plans to aid agricultural workers in developing countries go awry. How could it be otherwise when half those workers may as well be invisible?

In rural Kenya, thirty-six-year-old Fanisi Kalusa regularly rises at dawn in the small dwelling which the family of nine shares with two cows and a goat (the animals sleep in the kitchen).[1] Before making breakfast for the seven children and readying them for school, she must make a journey. For in this house there are no sinks with running water, no well in the back yard. Taking her three-gallon pail in hand, she trudges down the steep slope behind the house to gather water from the stream below. Each morning she makes half a dozen of these water-fetching trips.

In this she is not alone. Throughout the Third World, collecting and carrying water for domestic use is woman's work. It is always an arduous task and it can be a time-consuming one. In Burkina Faso (Upper Volta) during the dry season, for example, women must walk four kilometers to fill their water jugs. They return with muddy swamp water, all that is available then.

Like rural women in other poor countries, Ms. Kalusa

A Syrian woman fills her water jug, which she will carry back down a long, rocky hill.

must also make a number of daily journeys on foot to gather fuel to cook with. Lacking an electric or gas stove, she uses firewood to do her cooking. In India, where both wood and coal are scarce, animal dung is used as fuel. That, too, must be sought and gathered.

From eight until noon this Kenyan woman digs and weeds on her husband's land. At three-quarters of an acre it is a tiny plot by any standard, but she must coax it into providing most of the family's staples—maize, beans, and bananas. At noon she prepares lunch for the children returning from school. At mid-afternoon she heads for the local marketplace several miles from her home. There she trades some of the surplus from her vegetable garden for other food items she needs for making the family's dinner. Then she walks home to do the cooking.

Fanisi Kalusa is not counted as a member of her country's labor force.

Women and Food Production

Women produce half of the world's food.[2] In Africa, three-quarters, and in Asia one-half of the agricultural work is done by women. Yet, until this decade, census and labor statistics completely concealed this fact. As late as 1974, the census of Bangladesh placed women's participation in the national economy at 2.5 percent, a not unusual statistic for developing countries.[3] Why are the efforts of millions of working women missed in the statistics?

The answer is that in the overwhelming percentage of cases, Third World women do not receive cash in exchange for their labor. In Malawi and Botswana in Africa, for example, more than three-quarters of the women work on the land but receive no pay.[4] More likely than not, they work to produce what is eaten by their immediate families. Like Fanisi Kalusa, they exchange surplus produce for needed goods or services. Even when they do work in other people's fields for pay, it is often sporadic,

Left: *Mozambiquan migrant worker picking tea leaves.* Below: *women from Indonesia work up to their waists in a rice field. Harvesting crops is difficult physical labor.*

being necessarily interwoven with other domestic duties. Women's work contracts are usually negotiated informally and so the work easily escapes the official records.

It wasn't until 1982 that the United Nations provided a definition of labor which includes those activities that result in food and goods for home consumption and barter as well as those that yield a cash income. Furthermore, the United Nations properly and for the first time recognized as labor such women's domestic activities as water carrying, fuel gathering, and food processing.

The term "food processor" may well make you think of an electric machine that slices, dices, and purees food within seconds. But in the Third World, a food processor is apt to be a woman engaged in a task done by hand that is both fatiguing and time consuming. The job is vital. Not only does food processing prolong storage life. It is necessary for transforming many crops into edible form. Grains, for example, must be threshed and dried promptly after harvesting. To produce cooking oil, women must grind by hand the raw materials from which it is extracted: oil seeds, coconuts, or wild palm.

Rice (the grain eaten by more people worldwide than any other), maize, and cassava all need to be processed before they can be ingested. By husking and pounding, Third World women transform inedible grains into food. In Bangladesh women husk 70 percent of all the raw rice produced in that country. (Recall that they are said to be only 2.5 percent of the labor force.) In Africa, women also process cocoa, an export crop.

Food processing when done by hand is something Third World women do in their homes, an activity often sandwiched in between other domestic chores. Hand-processed sorghum is pounded with a pestle until the bran part of it is separated. When enough bran is removed, the grain is further pounded until it is a pulverized meal. How long does it take to process enough to eat? U.N. technologist Gary Whitbin reports that 9 pounds (4 kg) of sorghum are needed to feed a family of six and that it takes a woman pounding away at the grain three hours to produce this quantity.[5]

Some women spend much more time than this processing food, as much time as others spend working the land. For them, processing has become a source of income. But regardless of whether it is for home consumption or local use, food processing as an economic activity escapes mention in labor reports and statistics.

In places like Java in Indonesia, where hulling machines have replaced the need for hand pounding, women have lost a source of income.[6] In fact, the Green Revolution of the 1950s and 1960s, with its introduction of farm machinery including hullers, has generally tended to force rural women out of agriculture.

In almost all Third World countries, the various aspects of farm labor are divided by sex. There are "men's crops" (usually those for export) and "women's crops" (usually those for local consumption). Sometimes the cultivation of a single crop entails jobs assigned by sex. For example, in some places harvesting is exclusively men's work while in others it is considered women's work.

In the state of Kerala in southern India, the transplanting of rice is women's work. Kamala, a thirty-five-year-old woman with six children, works at transplanting seedlings in the rice fields of Kerala whenever the local planters are hiring. It is seasonal work since rice is raised twice a year here. Three months out of the year no employment is to be found in the fields.

The success of the crop depends on how well it is transplanted. It is important, but unenviable, work. Kamala describes it in her own words:

It is a messy and back-breaking job. One has to stand in mud and slush for hours together in rain or sun. . . . One can easily catch cold being exposed for long hours in such damp surroundings. . . . I present myself for work at 7:00 A.M. . . . Standing in ankle-deep water, I must bend down and pull out the rice saplings. . . . Every two minutes I pull out enough to make a bundle. Before I tie up the bundle I must free the saplings of all the mud and slush. The first half of the morning is spent in this operation, pulling out seedlings and bundling them up.

Transplanting starts around midday. I hold the bundle to be transplanted in one hand and transplant with the other hand, all the time bending forward. One plants three or four saplings at a time. If the field is well-puddled, I can finish my work at four o'clock.[7]

Then, like most women who work on the land, she begins her second work-shift at home—cleaning and preparing dinner.

It would be wrong though to think of Third World women doing only the messy, undesirable jobs in agriculture. In Nepal and in Ghana, studies show that women play important decision-making roles. They choose which seeds to plant and how much and what kind of fertilizers should be used.

Women and Technology

The governments of both Western and Third World countries frequently send agricultural technologists to poorer farming communities in order to introduce improved varieties of seed and planting techniques. In the past these advisers consistently sought out the men of these communities and ignored the women who do so much of the agricultural labor. Information and the operation of new equipment was targeted at men only.[8]

This has been a worldwide problem, one that was deplored by the U.N. Decade For Women. Only now are changes at last beginning to occur. In some places women farmers still get unequal attention. In Kenya, for example, "development" workers visit male farmers five times more frequently than they do female farmers cultivating the same crop. It's not a question of including a farmer's wife in the demonstration. In many parts of Africa and Asia women are frequently the heads of their households. According to one study in Kenya, nearly half of the district households studied were headed by a woman. Where are the husbands?

They have migrated to distant towns and cities in search of wage labor. Some return home at regular intervals; others have seemingly left for good. In Indonesia, "an estimated 60 percent of male migrants who seek work in the cities leave their families permanently."[9] Yet no single finding seems to be so consistent worldwide than the failure of development programs to reach women farmers. The U.N. Food and Agriculture Organization warns:

> In the Third World, agricultural production cannot be substantially increased nor can rural poverty be alleviated unless women's access to key production resources and services is substantially improved. The consequences of patriarchy for agricultural productivity are very expensive. Developing countries cannot bear their heavy cost.[10]

To begin righting the unfair distribution of technology and information by sex, the newly organized U.N. Development Fund For Women has initiated many fruitful projects. Through its funding, this group has also helped to extend successful projects previously developed on a small scale by other organizations.

An example of what is now happening thanks to the resources of the fund can be found in rural Jamaica. There women have begun to extract salt from the earth. This is a brand-new industry for the island. Its start-up required installation of relatively simple, inexpensive equipment, initially on a ten-acre site. It is a seasonal industry so that the women's labor is required only at certain times of the year. This suits their needs since most are also involved in other part-time income-producing activities.

In 1984, the first salt harvest produced and processed was one hundred tons. The success of the project led to plans for expanding the operation to an island-wide commercial venture that will eventually provide jobs for more Jamaican women and will make the country an exporter rather than an importer of salt.

The Fund For Women is also active in five countries of West Africa. Here in the coastal regions women are being taught how to smoke fish in a way that is improving both their profits and their health. During the three-month fishing season, men traditionally do the catching, women the marketing of what is caught. It is also the women's job to smoke the fish, a procedure necessary for extending its storage life. But the traditional methods they used were both wasteful and hazardous. The smoking process was done in thatched huts over wood fires. The job consumed many hours of a woman's day as well as much precious fuel. Damaging fires frequently resulted.

Women of Togo, Guinea, and Benin are now profiting from the invention of a new type of oven. It was invented in 1971 by the women of Chakor, Ghana, with the aid of technical assistance funds. It is inexpensive to build, lasts fifteen years, and smokes ten times the amount of fish with the same amount of fuel as the traditional smoker. And the fish lasts up to nine months!

In Swaziland, Africa, the Fund For Women has helped train two thousand rural women to produce machine-made goods for which there are ready local markets. It also offers women the use of a revolving loan fund which permits the trainees to buy the equipment and raw materials necessary for setting themselves up in business. Obtaining a loan is a most difficult achievement for rural women throughout the Third World. For although women work the land, invariably they do not *own* land and have no collateral. In many countries single women have the right to own land but they lose it upon their marriage. According to a United Nations report, "so complete is the disinheritance of women, that it has been estimated that they own less than one hundredth of the world's property."[11]

Systematically denied help from banks, Third World women are forced to turn to money lenders who charge exorbitant interest rates. The agricultural organizations of the United Nations believe that rural women have to find a way of gaining independent access to land and loans. They suggest that perhaps all-women cooperative farms are the key to their future liberation.[12]

7
WOMEN IN INDUSTRY

Look at a pocket calculator, a transistor radio, or a home computer. In all likelihood you are seeing a piece of machinery produced largely by women. It may come as a surprise, but in industries that depend on labor in Third World Countries—and in the electronics industry, especially—manpower is really womanpower. What is life like for a female factory worker in the Third World? Experience varies with country and industry.

Being a Female Factory Worker in Mexico, the Caribbean, and Latin America

If you are one of the hundreds of thousands of women who make up 75 percent of the assembly lines in Mexico, the Caribbean, and Latin America, you might be producing anything from baseballs to sophisticated electronic equipment.[1] Though management may assume that you are bringing home a secondary wage and that it is being spent on luxury items since your husband provides the bulk of the family's support, this assumption may well be wrong. Unlike the situation in the Orient where factory work is done largely by unmarried women between the ages of eighteen and twenty-four, here it is also done by low-income, older women with families to support. Indeed there is a good chance that you are the adult head of your household and the main provider for yourself and a number of dependent children. "In Haiti, 55 percent of women factory workers head households averaging seven people. In the apparel industry in Ciudad Juarez (in Mexico), approximately one out of every three women heads a household of seven. And these women put in 'double days,' running their household while holding down a full-time job."[2]

Your wages barely allow you and your family to live at the poverty level. If you have a teenage daughter, you will expect her to stay home from school to take care of the younger children during the day. You will put in a ten-hour day at the factory. Then you will take an hour-long bus ride home, stopping to shop for groceries before returning to cook dinner, do laundry, and put young children to bed. You do your job well, but you know that your chances of getting a promotion to a supervisory or managerial position are slim, again because it is assumed that higher paying jobs should go to men, who are assumed to be the primary wage earners.

Women and Industry

Women constitute "only one quarter of those employed in industry—in rich and poor countries alike. Their share of industrial jobs is growing, however, increasing from 24 to 28 percent between 1960 and 1980—largely as a result of the rapid expansion of industrial employment in parts of Asia."[3] Some of this expansion was due to the launching of indigenous industrial enterprises in the 1960s. Developing countries, newly independent of the colonial powers that had earlier introduced them to capitalist methods of production, sought at that time to compete with the rich nations for world markets. There was another important factor in Third World industrial expan-

Above: a worker at a sporting goods company sorts baseballs in one of several steamy factories in Haiti where 95 percent of American baseballs are manufactured. The job, performed mostly by women, pays about $3 a day, the cheapest wage rate in the Caribbean. Because of the extremely high unemployment rate in Haiti, a job in a baseball factory is very desirable. Facing page: a young Malaysian woman works diligently with a piece of silver jewelry.

sion—the skyrocketing price of oil during the 1970s. As a result, many Western companies moved part of their operations to Third World countries, lured there by lower taxes, less stringent labor laws, and cheap labor. The cheap labor being made available to them was largely that of young women. A foreign investment brochure quoted as typical in a 1981 *Ms.* report on multinational corporations makes this quite explicit: "The manual dexterity of the Oriental female is famous the world over. Her hands are small and she works fast with extreme care. . . . Who, therefore, could be better qualified by nature and inheritance to contribute to the efficiency of an assembly production line than the Oriental girl?"[4]

Women's participation in the industrial work force varies by country and industry. Some industries, particularly those located in the "free trade zones" of the Far East, employ more female than male workers. In Malaysia, for instance, "85 percent of people working in the Bayan Lepas free trade zone are women aged between eighteen and twenty four . . . and in Mauritius young women are 80 percent of the newly-hired free trade zone workers."[5] In Barbados, Tunisia, Puerto Rico, and El Salvador, women constitute roughly half the work force in the textile industry. And the tobacco industries of both Indonesia and Thailand employ more women than men.[6] This is an example of a "cottage industry" since women roll the tobacco in a piecemeal fashion in their own homes. In contrast, the strawberry export business brings young Mexican women out of their homes and villages. Since 1970, for example, the Mexican strawberry business, stimulated by U.S. investment and the American market, has employed about 10,000 young women in its packing plant in Zamora.

Apart from assembly line work, being a domestic is the only real job option open to the women of the Zamora region. Given the choice, those who are unmarried and between the ages of fifteen and twenty-four prefer to work in the packing plant. Their genial attitude toward factory work is one of the main reasons that multinational corporations in the Third World give 80 to 90 percent of their low-paying and semiskilled assembly line jobs to women. The personnel manager of one such corporation said: "Young male workers are too restless to do monotonous work with no career values. If displeased, they sabotage the machines and even threaten the foreman. But girls? At most they cry a little."[7]

Women are certainly as capable as men of fighting management, as the history of labor struggles in the West and in countries like South Africa shows.[8] But in Mexico and the Far East young women workers are preferred by companies where conditions make their organization unlikely, at least in the immediately foreseeable future. These young women "are willing to accept low wages, often because there is no other work available for them; they are docile, having been raised in societies where a husband's or father's word is obeyed without question . . . they are used to being allocated tedious, painstaking tasks at home; they tend to leave—or are fired—when they have children. . . . This high turnover also means that . . . few women are around long enough or are committed enough to a future in the factory, to push for better pay and conditions."[9]

Conditions in
Third World Factories

What conditions do female factory workers face? In the strawberry packing plants in Zamora, Mexico, the women either remove stems from the fruit or crate the already-stemmed strawberries. In 1980 they did these jobs for (U.S.) 66¢ per hour or (U.S) 25¢ per crate for an average monthly wage of (U.S.) $51.[10] The wages vary from month to month depending on the market value of the crop. There are no contracts, no fringe benefits, no social security. There is

also no work four months out of the year. When there is, the workday is ten hours long.

These women workers enjoy little freedom of movement. Twice daily they are escorted to and from the plant and the buses that transport them to their home villages in the outlying area. The fear is that left unchaperoned they would be harassed by men lurking in the streets of the town.

The 1981 *Ms.* report referred to earlier enumerates the severe health hazards faced by many female factory workers in the Third World. In Malaysia, the teenage girls and young women who make pocket calculators must peer into microscopes between seven and nine hours a day while bonding hair-thin wires of gold to a silicon chip. This is a job which after three years is likely to damage their eyesight. Elsewhere in the vast electronics industry, toxic chemicals in open containers fill the work area with fumes that sometimes overpower workers. And in the textile industry of the Third World, women sometimes work for three dollars a day amid dust that can cause respiratory diseases.

As mentioned earlier, the Western-managed multinational corporations are not the only companies involved in manufacturing in Third World countries. Many locally owned and managed firms are also involved, and in some countries, such as Hong Kong, Taiwan, and South Korea, and in some industries—such as the garment industry regardless of country—these companies, though usually smaller, outnumber the multinational ones. In these smaller, indigenously owned firms, "wages are usually lower and working conditions worse, sometimes much worse, than in the multinational sector."[11]

In Mexico City, a seamstress concentrates on her work.

Who Works and Why

A worldwide survey undertaken by the International Labor Organization (ILO) reported in 1985 that of the women employed in export-oriented multinational corporations, "between 70 and 95 percent are single, mostly never-married women. The typical worker is a young, unmarried woman in her late teens or early twenties. . . . It is in fact the explicit intention of most young, single women entering factory employment to work only a few years between school-leaving (or the minimum working age) and marriage."[12]

The strawberry packers of Zamora, Mexico, are predominantly young, unmarried women, but among them are also wives whose distantly settled husbands do not send enough money from the wages they earn to support the children. Most of the unmarried workers hand over their paychecks to their fathers. Their wages do not entirely support their families, but they are used for purchasing household consumer goods, most notably electric appliances. This, too, fits in with a wider pattern. The ILO survey shows that women factory workers in multinational corporations throughout the Third World typically hand over more than half of their earnings to parents if they live at home. Some turn over all their earnings. Deprived of the right to spend most of their wages as well as personal freedom, why do these women continue to work?

The answer is that they see no better alternatives. They also have a mental resiliency that allows them to see the bright side of things. Said one of Zamora's ace strawberry packers: "We don't mind being tired because we have earned our few pennies and have left the little ranch for a while. . . . In the village you get bored by seeing the same faces all day long and listening to the same gossip. By working we entertain ourselves"[13] It's a sentiment echoed as far away as Singapore. There factory women who have quit their jobs upon becoming housewives report that they miss the companionship of their female co-workers on the assembly line.[14]

The Service Sector

As countries expand industrially, more jobs are created not only in the factories themselves, but also in the service sector related to industry. Worldwide it is in the service sector—which includes secretaries, file clerks, and office cleaners—that women have the largest share of jobs: 27 percent in the Third World and half in the rich world.[15] Why are women so heavily employed in the service sector? One reason that has been given is that these jobs "dovetail so neatly with women's traditional domestic roles of supporting and cleaning up after men that they have quickly become seen as 'women's' jobs in most countries."[16]

What Will the Future Bring?

Although Third World women working in industry frequently make better wages than those working in agriculture or as maids (a major source of employment for Latin American women), they still face many problems and it is difficult to imagine how these will be eliminated in the foreseeable future. In those countries and industries with huge labor supplies to draw upon and relatively rapid turnover of employees (in the factories in Asia, for example), women are not in a good position to improve their situation.

On the positive side, the U.N. Decade for Women (1975–1985) "saw an increase in the number of countries—from twenty-eight in 1978 to ninety in 1983—holding equal pay legislation on their statute books, making it illegal to give men and women different wages for the same work."[17] Even so, women often find themselves in the kinds of jobs that are also among the lowest-paying (jobs as waitresses, secretaries, assembly-line workers, office cleaners, etc). As long as societies define these jobs as being the only ones suitable for women, young women will have little motivation to even imagine themselves doing anything else. Until women can compete equitably with men for better jobs, it is difficult to see how the cycle can be broken.

BEING IN BUSINESS

When you "go shopping" most likely you go to a store of some kind whether it's the corner grocery, a giant department store, or a suburban shopping mall. But in the Third World, people purchase most of the things they need in open air markets which seemingly spring to life out of nowhere and vanish again when shopping hours are over. And the people selling goods at these markets are invariably women. In West Africa, the Caribbean, and South Asia, the overwhelming majority of all farm and fishing products consumed locally is sold, as well as bought, by women.[1] And their wares are not limited to foodstuffs. There is hardly an item for sale in the market that the women don't handle.

The Life of a Market Woman

If you worked in one of the major markets of the large Nigerian city of Ibadan, you would spend much of your day in one of the hundreds of stalls in the long sheds that fill more than twelve acres. There you might be selling meat or fresh vegetables, fruit, cloth, jewelry, bedding, pottery, or ógún (traditional medicine).[2] Or you might sell manufactured goods like candles, hair cream, powdered

A roadside boutique in Egypt

milk, or canned goods. Or you might sell food that you cook right in your stall. You would spend a lot of your time shouting, mostly to advertise your wares, but also while bargaining with your customers. You have to shout because the place is so noisy. Your patrons, including those who don't know you, address you as "Madam" or "Mama." Both are terms of respect. Your clientele speak a variety of African languages, and you have found that it helps business to be able to speak a smattering of as many of these languages as possible.

You have to be alert at all times. It is easy to be robbed and you carry no theft or fire insurance. In any case, a robbery would be extremely difficult to prove. For one thing, you keep no written records of purchases for your stock or of your sales. You have never learned to read.

There are other worries to sabotage your sleep at night. Health officers can come by to inspect your operation at any time. They can easily condemn your little business and you can't afford the bribes they are after. You need money desperately, but you know that only the wealthy trading women can get credit lines. Loans are unthinkable; you have no collateral—no money, no land.

It is difficult to sleep for other reasons as well. You live in a housing compound with many other market women who, like yourself, are single or who, were abandoned by husbands. The apartments are tiny, poorly ventilated, and have no electricity. You have to use an oil lamp for light. There are communal bathing stalls shared by almost sixty people. Like half of the women living in the compound, you are the head of your household. That means you are the sole supporter of your children.

But if you were to compare your life with that of a female factory worker, you would feel relatively lucky. You would be quick to point out the independence that a marketing life affords. You work longer hours and for lower wages at times, but you are responsible to no one but yourself. There is the companionship of your neighboring stall-keepers, who form a kind of mutual aid society and support group. Most importantly, you needn't be separated from your children during the day as is the case with factory workers. You just bring them along to your stall, nursing them while they are infants, feeding and watching over them when they are older. Eventually, when your daughters come of age, you will initiate them into the "fine art" of retail marketing.

In Lima, the capital of Peru, more than 47,000 small traders conduct business in 290 marketplaces throughout the city, and many of them are women.[3] About half of these markets are permanent. The others are set up temporarily in open lots or on the streets. Renting a stall in one of the permanent markets is more desirable because they have space for storage and refrigeration. Also, the city of Lima controls them and is responsible for keeping the spaces clean and secure.

In addition to dozens of varieties of fresh and prepared foods and spices, the Lima market vendors sell baskets, shoes, thread, yarn, and radios. You can even find television repair here!

Sociologist Ximena Bunster B. interviewed twenty-one Lima market women between the ages of twenty-one and fifty-three to learn something of their lives. Most, she discovered, were illiterate and had an average of three years of primary schooling. Here, as in Africa, they tended not to operate the kinds of businesses that required a lot of money. The meat stalls, for example, with their need for refrigerators, were operated by men.

The women start their day at 3:00 A.M., leaving their homes two hours later. At about 6:30 they open their stands and set up their wares. Then they are joined by their school-aged children, who have breakfast with them at the marketplace before going to school.

The busiest hours are in the morning. At 1:00 P.M. sales drop off sufficiently for the women to take lunch; they always eat on the premises. When the Lima markets close at 5:00 P.M., the women return to their homes to cook the evening meal, wash and iron clothes, and put the children to bed.

The biggest complaint they have is lack of sleep. But like their African counterparts, they praise the market way of life. Many of the women had previously worked in agriculture, as domestics, or as street vendors. The marketplace was, for them, a step upward. One of the women described it as "a window on the world." And they echoed the African women's view that it is a job with enough

A busy, open-air market
in Guatemala

built-in flexibility to make some degree of child care possible. Children here start helping their mothers behind the counter at the age of ten, relieving them when a younger child, sick at home, needs their attention.

Nevertheless, the women have serious problems and the markets, for all their color and conviviality, should not be romanticized. They are often unsanitary places since garbage is not collected daily. The lavatories are frequently unclean. The weather is often bad so that the women who work in the stalls can expect to suffer from colds and bronchitis.

They face other problems, too. Wholesalers hoard scarce products, and the more prosperous retailers—those with storage space—buy them up. Poorer women must buy only what they can sell in a given time. Their children are often exhausted in school because they have been up the whole night before, having accompanied their mother to a wholesaler to help transport sacks of vegetables needed for the following day's business.

Inspectors intimidate even those who have broken no laws with threats of jail or the forced removal of their wares. And those whose job it is to help small entrepreueners often refuse to assist these outdoor traders. In fact, Ximena Bunster B. concludes that, in general, city authorities view the work of market people as not quite legitimate. She says that their "ramshackle stalls are seen as an affront to modernization."

The Tycoons

It would be wrong to get the idea that in the Third World all businesswomen are small traders living on the brink of poverty. Some have climbed to the very pinnacle of the magic mountain of big business. Although they are a tiny minority, no account, however brief, of Third World women in business would be complete without a look at their achievements. Table 3 compares the achievement of se-

Table 3
Percentage of Female and Male
Workforce in Administrative and
Managerial (Bosses) and
Clerical (Secretaries) Jobs

	BOSSES		SECRETARIES	
	Women	Men	Women	Men
GERMANY (West)	1.3	4.2	34.0	9.6
HUNGARY	0.1	0.2	16.4	3.5
NORWAY	2.0	6.6	26.0	2.5
UNITED STATES	3.8	10.4	27.9	5.5
JAPAN	0.4	6.4	18.2	9.4
*EGYPT	0.8	0.9	25.0	6.5
*BAHRAIN	0.4	1.1	46.0	5.8
*SINGAPORE	1.2	8.2	14.9	5.7
*VENEZUELA	1.6	9.2	16.7	7.6

*Third World countries (asterisks added by author).

Source: *Women: A World Report,* Debbie Taylor, ed. (New York: Oxford University Press, 1985), p. 36.

lected groups of women in a number of developing and developed countries.

A recently published series of interviews with four highly successful Thai women executives show that they share certain key characteristics.[4] Not surprisingly, they are hard workers with a sensitivity to the importance of human relations. But perhaps more importantly, all are daughters or granddaughters of the founders of the large companies they currently manage. Significantly, all are married and have children. Their husbands are also successful executives who endorsed their professional ambitions from the start. All had an excellent education, including university training, and admitted that this was an essential ingredient in their success.

Like the less privileged women we have met so far, these executives feel they must juggle professional and domestic responsibilities. Sometimes the conflict between the two seems very great to them. Chatchani Chatikavanij, one of the women interviewed, chairs a group of Thai companies that produces items ranging from cooking oil to sophisticated electronic equipment. She says: "Admittedly many successful businesswomen do not have a successful family life because a married career woman is simultaneously holding down two jobs. She can't neglect either and she has to do them equally well. If the husband doesn't demand too much, she can achieve both without too much pressure."

Another of the interviewees was Ms. Phornthip Narongdei, thirty-six-year-old vice president of a Thai automobile company. She admitted that her definition of success, at least for herself, was an impossible one to attain because it included "being a perfect mother, a perfect wife, a perfect daughter, perfect sister, perfect boss . . ."

Ms. Sunandha Tulayadhan, the thirty-seven-year-old manager of the Southeast Asia office of Ogilvy and Mather, a giant American advertising firm, gives this advice to Thai women seeking a career in big business: "Set your priorities straight. If you have a lot of other obligations, i.e., young children, then you must decide whether you want to be a successful woman or be a good mother."

Although these female executives are exceptional, there is evidence that in general, women in Thailand are increasingly finding jobs in management. During the period from 1968 to 1981, about two-thirds of the undergraduates receiving degrees in accounting and finance at three of Bangkok's leading universities were women. Furthermore, a little under half of the 1,390 Thai students who initially participated in a new American program that grants a master's degree in business administration were female.[5] An explanation that has been offered for the unusually high rate of women pursuing business careers in Thailand is that in this country men see entry into civil service as the most realistic substitute for becoming a monk, the position that for Theravada Buddhists is the ideal career for men. Jobs in business are regarded as being too obviously "of this world" and are left to a larger degree than elsewhere to women.[6]

Despite their significance as small traders in West Africa, the Caribbean, and South Asia, women worldwide are underrepresented in the realm of big business. Yet some have made it to the top, even in places where they have long been trained to keep their noses to the domestic grindstone. One such place is Egypt, where against all odds there is however small a female entrepreneurial elite. In 1976, only 1.7 percent of the female Egyptian labor force was employed in executive, administrative, or managerial positions.[7] (This is actually a higher rate than for the United States in 1982 when only an estimated 1 percent of employed women held managerial positions.)[8] But among this group were women who either head the Egyptian office of large, multinational corporations like U.S. Steel, Nestle's, Alcoa, and General Motors, or themselves own large businesses employing thousands of workers.

In 1983, writer Earl Sullivan profiled twelve of Egypt's successful businesswomen and discovered that they shared certain characteristics.[9] Typically, they were in their mid-fifties and had been in business for no more than twelve years. All had received a good education and were multilingual. All but one was from a big city such as Cairo or Alexandria.

Like their counterparts in Thailand, these women came from wealthy families active in business or politics. All of them felt that their background had given them a certain self-confidence and assertiveness, personality traits they considered vital for success in business.

Their mothers had married young even before finishing their basic schooling. The tycoons themselves had married at the age of about nineteen, the average for their generation. They had gone on to have an average of two children and had spent a good proportion of their lives as housewives. A period ranging from twelve to thirty-five years elapsed between the time of their marriages and the start-up of their businesses.

As in the case of the successful Thai women, the husband's role was critical. Most of these women said they learned their business skills from their husbands, initially in an unintentional way. They had simply absorbed the "shoptalk" that always seemed to invade their husbands' conversation, particularly when they were socializing with colleagues. Sometimes the husbands took a more active role, helping their wives to set up a business.

The case of Ms. S. was different. In 1961, her husband became a political prisoner and was unable to run his large advertising firm. She recalls:

> I was left with two children, a newly established advertising company and no money. I had to manage my life. My oldest brother . . . and my sister did not appreciate my working. They rejected (the idea of) my working, meeting people, and travelling. But I had to earn a living by any means.[10]

Although she had no prior experience in the field of advertising, she was personable, spoke a number of languages, and was quick to learn. She did so well that when her husband was released and able to resume work, he took another job and she retained control of the firm. Twenty-five years later it is one of the largest and most successful advertising agencies in Egypt and Ms. S. still heads it.

What is the biggest problem faced by these successful Egyptian businesswomen? The answer is, in the words of one of them is: "credibility. . . . You have to be ten times as good as a man to convince people that you are good. I keep my promises religiously, scrupulously. . . . Any benefit of doubt goes to the other person—customer, employee, whatever—just to prove that the word I say is as good as a contract. Many men can get by with less than that. They can promise things they forget at once . . ."[11]

Do these women tend to hire female workers to a greater degree than men in their position? Not at all. They say they don't want to fight the stereotype that would surely mark them if they did. In general, they feel that being businesswomen, they have enough of a fight on their hands as it is.

Mention must also be made of those whom the African journalist Elanga Shungu has dubbed "The Mercedes Ladies."[12] These are nine very successful female entrepreneurs of the city of Lomé in Togo. Their great wealth has earned them the title of "Nana," which does not mean "grandma" but rather "chief" in Mina, their native language. How did these African women become rich enough to be chauffeured in limousines and vacation in style on the French Riviera?

Described as a close-knit, though competitive, group, they have managed to nearly corner the European market for West African fabrics. With the profits from their sales, they are now expanding into other businesses: jewelry, home appliances, restaurants, bakeries, and supermarkets. They are also investing their profits in real estate ventures, particularly in renting homes to non-African employees of multinational corporations who must relocate in Togo.

The backgrounds of these women contrast sharply with the other successful businesswomen we have met. Most of them are illiterate. Nevertheless, they are able to deal effectively with both their foreign customers and the banks that handle their multimillion-dollar accounts.

Profile: Maria—
A Portrait of Determination

The case of banking executive Maria B. of the Dominican Republic is quite different from those we have encountered so far. Though it, too, is a success story, this success is due neither to privileged background nor to a marketing coup, but rather to inner drive, hard work, and perseverance.

Born in 1940, the daughter of a Dominican jazz musician, Maria grew up in a small town on the island. Her father's band was brought there by Rafael Trujillo, ruler of the Dominican Republic from 1942 until 1952. At the time he wished to make the town a center of cultural activity as well as the seat of island government.

Maria attended a local Catholic girls' school from first grade through high school. Then she wished to study law, but her family had other ideas. At the age of eighteen, she was sent abroad to live with an aunt in Boston. There she spent a year, attending night classes at a secretarial school where she tried to master shorthand in a language she barely understood. This proved most frustrating, and there were times, she recalls, when to save her life she could not have read back what she had written in shorthand. But she persevered and mastered English as well as typing and shorthand within the year. Then she returned home.

Jobs there were scarce. Despite her new skills it was difficult to find office work of any kind. She recalls: "Finally I got a job in the U.S. Navy Office. But two months later, my country practically declared war on America. The Navy left the Dominican Republic and I was again out of work!"

Shortly thereafter, Maria decided to go to Puerto Rico. There she found work with a broker of Swiss watches. Much of his business was with the United States and he was happy to have an English-speaking secretary. It was a low-paying job, but Maria stayed with it for three years. Then she worked as a secretary for an insurance company, later for a laboratory. Then, homesick, she returned to the Dominican Republic.

There she married an agricultural engineer and began to raise a family of four children, including a set of twin girls. She was, however, determined to continue working and to find a better job. Her mother-in-law, who lived two doors away, took care of the youngsters during the day. Her husband was unhappy with this arrangement, but saw that his wife would have it no other way.

In 1967, Maria obtained a position at First National City Bank office in Santo Domingo, the capital of the Dominican Republic and the city where she now lived. She says:

That was the beginning of my life in the banking world. I started as a secretary to the operations manager. I realized it would be helpful if I knew accounting. At that time I didn't know a debit from a credit. I went to the manager and said: "I want to learn this business of accounting but I can't seem to find the beginning of it."

He handed me a big, black book and said: "Learn everything in this book and you'll know what it's all about." I read that manual—very slowly—and that's how I began to learn accounting. After that I came to work in succession for three different bosses, each more important in the organization. The last taught me a great deal. Then there came a point when he said: "I don't know what to do with you now."

Maria had reached the position of assistant accountant, but had, in fact, become overqualified for even this job. The solution came when a new building was to be constructed. Maria was placed in charge of the bank's accounting office responsible for maintenance and construction. She was sent to New York to deliberate with the architects and engineers involved in the bank's building projects throughout the world.

When the new building was completed, Maria was transferred to the "technology products department." The goal of this division was to sell new technology to companies in the Dominican Republic.

This was my introduction to the computer world. In order to sell the hardware, I had to know how to use it. So I learned how to use all kinds of different computers. But this project was doomed. It's not yet the time to sell computers in a country like the Dominican Republic. But I learned a great deal in the meantime.[13]

Maria had by this time worked nineteen years for the bank. She explains that American companies do not offer Dominican employees retirement plans, only a bonus when they leave after fifteen years or more of service. Is she thinking of retiring from work? Definitely not. A new locally-owned bank opened in 1985 with the promise of higher pay and more fringe benefits. There was a position for an executive accountant and Maria decided she was their woman. She was. Today she works for that bank and happily speaks of being in on the ground floor of a new, expanding enterprise. She is also putting her eldest daughter through college in New York, where she is studying marketing.

⑨
ENTERING THE PROFESSIONS

The great majority of Third World women who support themselves and their children do so by working on the land, in factories, or at the market stalls. But a tiny percentage—through a combination of factors that include financial resources, connections, the social conditions of their country, perseverance, and a bit of luck—have succeeded in getting the kind of higher education that has enabled them to become doctors, lawyers, teachers, and other professionals. Table 4 indicates the prevalence of female professionals and administrators in various developing and developed countries.

Little has been written about this group, although its influence may be proportionately greater than its size. One reason may be that nowadays the highly educated citizens of Third World countries frequently emigrate if they are determined to practice their chosen profession. Poor countries such as India have developed medical schools that attract their young people, but the country cannot compete with Western nations in providing satisfying work opportunities for its graduates. From Argentina to the Philippines, the mass exodus of college-trained young people to the United States, Canada, and Great Britain has been dubbed the "brain drain." Most typically it involves the emigration of young, professionally trained men.

Table 4
Percentage of Total Population of Each Sex in Professional and Administrative Occupations, 1980(a) and Percentage of Total Labor Force in Industry, 1980(b)

Country (or area)	(a) M	(a) F	(b) M	(b) F
*Afghanistan	1	0	3	0
Australia	10	5		
*Bahrain	7	3	11	3
*Bangladesh	1	0		
*Barbados	7	5		
Bulgaria	9	11		
*Cameroon	2	0	3	1
Canada	12	9		
*El Salvador	2	1	5	8
French Polynesia	5	4		
Germany (West)	10	5		
*Guyana	23	8	43	39
Hong Kong	6	3	13	10
*Indonesia	1	1	8	6
*Iran	2	1	6	0
Ireland	6	4		
Israel	9	8	8	9
Japan	7	4	27	15
*Kuwait	8	4	10	2
*Mali	1	0	1	0
*Nepal	2	1		
Netherlands	10	5		
New Zealand	10	6		
Norway	13	10	6	13
*Panama	5	4	4	5
*Philippines	2	3	4	6
Portugal	3	3	9	7
Puerto Rico	12	7	8	8

Table 4 (Cont.)

Country	(a)		(b)	
(or area)	M	F	M	F
*Seychelles	4	4		
*Singapore	8	4	14	12
*Sri Lanka	2	2	7	1
Sweden	15	15		
*Syria	4	1	7	1
*Thailand	2	1	4	5
*Turkey	5	2		
*United Arab Emirates	6	3	12	1
United States	16	9	7	16
*Venezuela	5	4	9	6

*Third world countries (asterisks added by author).

Source: Women: A World Report, Debbie Taylor, ed. (New York: Oxford University Press, 1985), p. 361.

Two of the three women profiled in this chapter found themselves in a predicament similar to that of their male fellow graduates. In their cases, they had to come to the United States to complete their education, and then they decided to stay in order to pursue their careers.

Whatever the differences in the conditions under which the three women grew up, one common thread runs through their lives. Their families, including their fathers, saw education as essential and they encouraged the women to get all the education they could.

This attitude is behind the professional success of the members of certain ethnic groups in the United States as well. Many of the people in these groups came here with little more than a respect for the value of education. In earlier decades of this century, it was Jewish immigrants. More recently it has been Cuban immigrants, and more recently still, Asians.

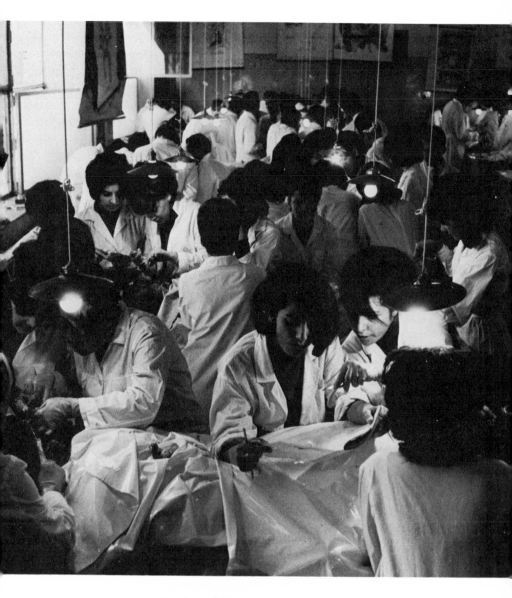

*Medical students in a lab at Teheran
University, Iran. The men and women students
are divided into separate groups.*

Profile: May—"Don't Throw Away Your Knowledge"

May was born in Manila, the capital of the Philippines, in 1940. She attended a private Catholic school from kindergarten through high school. Schooling was a subject never far from her consciousness. Her father, a retired army man, was deeply involved financially as well as personally in a project initiated and managed by May's mother's family: the building and eventually the maintenance of a school. So the energies of May's parents, as well as her maternal aunts and uncles, were, as far back as she can recall, geared toward furthering education. One aunt in particular—May's mother's sister—was the guiding force behind the project. Says May: "The memory of this woman's ambition and drive was to exert a powerful influence on me in later years. She in particular made me want to strive to always do the best that I could. But, of course, it was my mother who really set me on the course of my present life."

May never doubted that she would one day attend college. She took her degree, at St. Paul's College in Manila, in the field of nutritional science. But upon completing her degree she and her classmates discovered that there were no jobs to be gotten in which they could utilize their knowledge. Disheartened by this situation, May's college friends turned to other jobs. Her female friends became airline attendants and May began to think of becoming one herself. At this point her mother intervened. According to May she said: "Don't throw away your knowledge no matter what others are doing. We'll somehow find a way to help you." She proceeded to raise the money necessary for sending her daughter to a university in the United States, where May earned a master's degree in nutritional science. With it she landed a position as director of the Food Services Division of a large American hospital. Except for brief visits back home to visit her family and to marry, May has lived and worked here ever since.

She is in charge of 150 employees and is responsible for managing the hospital's $1.5 million food budget. "I worry about this operation quite a lot," she says. "It's a big job and very demanding, but it's also very fulfilling. I know that I'm one of the lucky ones. I have a husband who is supportive of my working and who understands not only the pressures of my job but also my love of this work. And I have a family that made it possible for me to be here."[1]

Halfway around the world in southern Africa, apartheid has made higher education and a livelihood in the professions far more difficult for black women to achieve. Still, some have managed to do the seemingly impossible.

Profile: Lindawe
Helping Others From Afar

Lindawe was born in 1958 in what is now called Harare and was then called Salisbury, the capital of the African Republic of Zimbabwe, formerly Southern Rhodesia. Zimbabwe became an independent state in 1980. Until she was eighteen years old, Lindawe, a black African, lived in a country ruled by whites who formed less than 4 percent of the country's total population. This had been the situation for the better part of a century.

In 1930, the British government which ruled Rhodesia reserved half of the total land area of the country—including all the mining and industrial areas—for white settlers. The other half of the land, including some towns and some areas within white-settled cities, were allocated to the native blacks, who constituted 96 percent of the population.[2] A tiny minority of 0.5 percent of the country are today either of Asian background or are referred to as "colored" and are the products of interracial couplings.

Lindawe, the first-born of three children, spent much of her childhood in the black ghetto of the capital. Her father, who had a degree from a South African Institute for black African men, worked as personnel manager for a big company. Her mother was a nurse in a hospital. Lindawe spent her first year of schooling at a government-run school for black African children. Her parents were so appalled by its lack of facilities and the poor quality of education offered that they entered her the following year in a private "multiracial school," the term used for schools set up for black and colored Africans.

In 1967 an extraordinary offer was made to Lindawe's mother. She had long wanted to become a teacher of nurses and now she was being given the opportunity to enter a teacher-training program for medical people that was to take place in England. Lindawe's father, who saw education as the key to independence for the country as well as for individuals, supported her leaving. So it was that Lindawe's mother left Africa; she was not to return for eight years. In the meantime, her place in the household was taken by her own sister, Lindawe's favorite aunt.

During the years that followed, Lindawe and her brother and sister spent their summer vacations with their father's parents, who lived in "tribal trust land," that part of the countryside where black Africans were allowed to live. There Lindawe learned from her grandmother the skills taught to rural young women: the sowing, hoeing, and grinding of grains; cooking; and washing clothes. She also spent much time hauling water and firewood. Said her grandmother: "Just in case you marry a country man, you've got to learn to carry a bucket!"

But her father had different ideas. Lindawe remembers him as being "very strict. He had very high ambitions for me. At school I got good grades and he realized I had the potential for getting a college education. Even when I was very young he made sure I got books instead of toys for my birthday. When I reached thirteen, he was afraid that I might discover boys and sex and that he wouldn't know how to handle even talking about these things with me since it is taboo for fathers and daughters to discuss such matters here." Afraid, too, that I might be led to an early marriage—which he did not want for me—he sent me off at thirteen to an all-girl Catholic convent boarding school in the capital."

This was in the early 1970s, a turbulent time for the country. Rhodesia, seeking its independence from Great Britain, was sharply divided on what type of government the new state should have. Black Rhodesians wanted to see the establishment of majority rule whereas the tiny white minority wished to retain its dominance. Guerrilla warfare would continue until the cease-fire of 1980 when the new state of Zimbabwe was born and black African Robert Mugabe was elected its prime minister.

Says Lindawe: "In the 1970s there were only a handful of black Africans at Salisbury convent. I experienced a great deal of racial discrimination there. It was so unpleasant I had no intention of finishing, thinking I could always become a nurse. But a friend of mine knew about scholarships from schools in the U.S. and she gave me a form to fill out. As a result, I received a scholarship from Skidmore College where I took a degree in business administration. After that I did my master's at Fordham in Political Economy and Development."

While going to school in New York, Lindawe met a Zimbabwe man who is now her husband. They have a daughter, whom they sent back to Zimbabwe for one year when she was an infant so that Lindawe could finish her graduate degree. After completing her studies Lindawe worked at a number of temporary jobs. Early in 1987 she applied for an internship with the U.N. Development Fund For Women. It seemed a stepping stone to the career she wanted, but offered no pay, so the problem of child care again arose. It was decided to bring from Zimbabwe a young niece of her husband's who wanted to come to the United States. They are now a household of four and Lindawe has a paying job as a consultant at the U.N. She spends most of her working hours evaluating proposals for projects that would assist southern African women. She is particularly concerned about the lack of female-owned and managed businesses in southern Africa. She says: "Many of the things southern African women make are worthy of international markets, but historically these women have not had the experience that West African women have had in marketing. What we're trying to do here is assist small businesses run by women by training them to become more efficient managers and teaching them the fundamentals of export marketing."

Lindawe makes her home in New York, but she points out that in recent years women have risen to important posts in her country. The ambassador to Sweden is a woman, and there are several female ministers and deputy ministers in the new government. Ms. Nhongo, best known to people in Zimbabwe by the name she went by when she was a guerrilla leader, a name meaning "Spilled Blood," is now the minister heading the Ministry of Development and Women's Affairs. That such a bureau now exists is evidence, says Lindawe, of a new recognition on the part of government to improve the status of the nation's women.

Profile: Lee Tai-young— Pioneer of Legal Justice

In Korea the need to improve women's status was first brought to public attention by women's societies which began to appear in the second decade of this century. It was in that period, in 1915, that Lee Tai-young, the country's first female lawyer, was born.

Her father had died when she was two and, as was the custom, she and her mother moved immediately into the household of her mother's eldest married brother. It was here that she spent her growing-up years. "He was always exhorting me to become a lawyer when I grew up," she recalled in an interview with journalist David Finkelstein.[3]

But she did not immediately fulfill this wish, which also became her own, although she did graduate from Korea's Ehiva University, one of the largest in the world for women. For the ten years following her graduation she taught home economics at a girls' high school and also worked as a seamstress. She had to in order to support her household which by then included her four small children and, as was the custom, her mother-in-law. During those years her husband, who was later to become a high-ranking government official, was imprisoned in Japan for his activities in the Korean independence movement. When he was released at the end of World War II in 1945, he returned and urged his wife to undertake her long-suppressed desire to study law.

So it was that Lee Tai-young became Korea's first woman lawyer. She became a lecturer in law at the university that she had attended as a student, but she also began a remarkable practice. In 1957, with some of the income that she earned from teaching, she rented part of a small office in the city of Seoul and hung up her shingle. It read: Women's Legal Aid Center.

Describing its beginnings as a "one-desk operation," Ms. Lee says her goals were twofold: to fight divorce and inheritance laws that were unfair to women and to fight the equally prejudicial wage laws of the time. In that first year she handled 149 cases.

Twenty-five years and more than 100,000 cases later, her sign hung on a six-story building constructed with funds donated by the women of Korea. Today the center's staff consists of seven full-time and two part-time legal counselors. They specialize in cases of divorce, parent-child relations, adoption, and inheritance as well as criminal cases involving adultery, rape, assault, and fraud.

In the late 1970s Ms. Lee added a "mobile legal aid unit" to her facilities. The unit, based in a jeep, aims to reach impoverished women needing legal assistance who live in the outlying slum districts and cannot easily get to the Seoul office. Ms. Lee herself often rides in the jeep.

Described as a gentle person, Lee Tai-young has on occasion been an outspoken critic of the highest government officials of her country. Her ideas "made her an enemy of President Park Chung Hee, who had her arrested. In 1977, she was given a three-year suspended sentence and seven-year disbarment."[4]

Now a grandmother of ten, as well as one who has addressed Harvard Law School students, Ms. Lee is still working hard: writing books, serving on committees, doing everything she can, in her words, "to further peace and harmony in the home through justice and equality."

10

GETTING HEALTH CARE

The British statesman Benjamin Disraeli said, in a public speech on July 24, 1877, "The health of the people is really the foundation upon which their happiness and their powers as a state depend." A century later, the connections he made between health, happiness, and power have a special relevance to Third World women. Their health needs cannot properly be considered in a vacuum, because they are intimately tied to matters of written and customary law and to questions of political power. These women must quickly gain access to resources that will ensure their improved health. The need is urgent, for nothing less than the worldwide health of the next generation, both male and female, is at stake.

Malnutrition

As we've already seen, in some countries differences in health care for males and females begin in infancy. Girl babies are given less food than boys and are less likely to be taken to doctors and hospitals when they are ill. This is a pattern that continues for the rest of their lives.

In India, for example, a recent survey by the National Committee on the Status of Women revealed that in nearly

*A five-year-old Iranian boy attended by
a nurse and his mother. Often, girls do not
get this attention when they are sick.*

half of the families studied, males eat first and females eat whatever is left over. Often their meals consist of nothing more than scraps.[1] In Bangladesh, women may go for days with almost nothing to eat.[2] Another survey done in India showed that while the incidence of diseases caused by malnutrition is higher in women, the hospital rate of admission for boys and adult males suffering from these diseases is higher.[3] In Nepal, women are 50 percent more likely than men to go blind as a result of chronic lack of food.[4]

In some parts of Africa, women and children are subject to certain food taboos. These are rules that say women and children are not allowed to eat specified foods, usually protein-rich items such as chickens and eggs.[5]

Malnutrition is a major problem for women of the Third World. According to the best statistics, "two-thirds of women in Asia, half of African women, and a sixth of women in Latin America have nutritional anemia caused by the lack of the right kind of food."[6]

Maternal and Infant Mortality

A pattern of life-long undernourishment has disastrous effects when a woman becomes pregnant. The daily requirement established for pregnant women is 2,500 calories, but in India those who are impoverished consume, on the average, only 1,440 calories, according to that country's National Institute of Health.[7] As a result, in India, anemia during pregnancy accounts for one-sixth of maternal deaths during childbearing.[8] (See Table 5.)

In Bangladesh, anemia combined with poor prenatal care causes thousands of mothers to die in childbirth each year.[9] In 1980, the International Fertility Research Program estimated that "maternal mortality is up to ten times higher in developing countries than in developed ones."[10] In Africa and Asia alone, childbirth accounts for the annual deaths of half a million women[11] (See Table 6.) Why?

—132—

Being overworked and undernourished are not the only reasons. Throughout the Third World, poor women run enormous risks in becoming pregnant. As recently as the 1970s, 25 percent of Brazil's women "had no right to medical care for childbirth under the government's social welfare laws. Even when labor pains have already started, this 25 percent must go from one hospital to another before they are finally admitted."[12] In Brazil 80 percent of maternal deaths in childbearing are caused by either hemorrhage or infection.

It is not a problem peculiar to Brazil. According to the U.N. World Health Organization, more than half of the infants born in poor countries—80 percent in Africa and 90 percent in rural India—are delivered by attendants with no training in sanitary techniques.[13]

Infant mortality, like maternal mortality, is high in developing countries. In some districts of Gambia, West Africa, it averages 15 percent of all births.[14] In South Africa, according to 1970 government statistics, the infant mortality rate was 20.9 per 1,000 births among whites, but 110 per 1,000 births among blacks.[15] In developing countries, "low birth weight is by far the greatest single hazard for infants, increasing their vulnerability to development problems and death. Of all infant deaths, two-thirds occur among those weighing less than 2,500 grams [5.5 lbs.] at birth."[16] What causes fatally low birth weight in infants? A lifetime of undernourishment in the mothers. Women in developing countries often do not gain even the minimum recommended weight during their pregnancies. In parts of Africa, impoverished women actually lose weight during the last three months of pregnancy. (See Table 7.)

Contraception and Abortion

Despite the great hazards to their own lives and those of their infants, Third World women continue to satisfy the demands that they reproduce frequently. In rural Bangla-

Table 5
Percentage of Pregnant and Non-Pregnant Women with Nutritional Anemia

Country (or area)	Pregnant	Non-pregnant
Algeria	65	
Argentina	61	34
Bangladesh	66	70
Barbados		45
Bolivia		15
Botswana		20
Brazil	20	8
Burma	55	
Cape Verde	42	
Chile	32	3
Colombia	22	6
Costa Rica	44	30
Dominica	46	60
Egypt	75	
El Salvador	15	
Ethiopia	6	8
Fiji	68	72
Gambia	80	80
Ghana	64	
Guatemala	34	
Nepal	33	
Nicaragua	20	
Niger	57	36
Nigeria	65	50
Pakistan	65	
Papua New Guinea	55	
Peru	35	22
Philippines	47	37
Sierra Leone	45	
Singapore	26	
*South Africa	25	12
Guinea Bissau	85	85
Guyana	55	41

Table 5 (Cont.)

Country (or area)	Pregnant	Non-pregnant
India	68	60
Indonesia	65	55
Iran	50	
*Israel	29	29
Ivory Coast	34	
Jamaica	24	
Jordan		25
Kenya	48	
Laos	62	
Lebanon	50	44
Libya	47	24
Malawi	49	
Malaysia	77	
Mali	50	
Mauritania	24	
Mauritius	80	70
Mexico	38	17
Morocco	46	
Sri Lanka	62	
Tanzania	59	
Thailand	48	
Togo	47	
Trinidad & Tobago	56	21
Tunisia	38	31
Turkey	74	
Uganda	35	46
Uruguay		7
Venezuela	52	18
Zambia	60	
Zimbabwe	27	

*Non-Third World countries (asterisks added by author).

Source: Women: A World Report, Debbie Taylor, ed. (New York: Oxford University Press, 1985), p. 366.

Table 6
Maternal Mortality Rate
Per 100,000 Live Births

Country (or area)	1970	1980
*Angola	113.4	
*Argentina		84.5
Australia	24.5	8.1
Austria	25.8	12.7
*Bahamas	93.9	61.6
*Barbados	143.4	69.7
Belgium	20.4	10.6
Bulgaria	44.7	12.6
Canada	20.2	6.4
*Cape Verde		134.0
*Chile	179.1	66.0
*Costa Rica	112.5	49.0
*Cuba	70.5	45.7
Czechoslovakia	22.3	12.9
Denmark	8.5	11.8
*Ecuador	229.8	198.5
*Egypt	107.4	84.8
*Fiji	57.9	40.7
Finland	7.7	7.6
France		15.7
Germany (East)	44.7	23.4
Germany (West)	52.2	22.0
Greece	28.3	14.0
Guadeloupe	74.5	106.4
*Guatemala	157.0	120.8
*Guyana	63.3	153.4
Hong Kong	19.0	8.6
Hungary	39.5	15.5
Iceland	46.8	
Ireland	32.6	11.7
Israel	22.3	10.6
Italy	52.9	24.1
*Jamaica	105.6	

Table 6 (Cont.)

Country (or area)	1970	1980
Japan	51.6	22.9
*Jordan	46.9	49.8
*Kenya	203.9	
*Kuwait	19.9	14.9
Luxembourg	66.5	24.5
Malta	18.0	68.2
*Mauritius	171.1	99.4
*Mexico	143.0	108.2
Netherlands	12.1	6.9
New Zealand	30.5	11.5
Norway	12.4	13.6
*Panama	135.1	90.5
*Paraguay	159.5	
*Philippines	149.9	141.6
Poland	28.0	14.6
Portugal	54.4	42.9
Puerto Rico	28.1	5.3
Romania	129.3	129.2
*Singapore	31.4	7.4
South Africa	90.1	
Spain	32.2	13.0
Sweden	10.0	1.0
Switzerland	23.2	11.1
*Trinidad & Tobago	135.7	78.9
UK	18.0	11.6
*Uruguay	83.8	58.6
USA	21.5	9.6
*Venezuela	92.1	65.1
Yugoslavia	53.4	14.6
*Zimbabwe	45.8	

*Third World countries (asterisks added by author).

Source: Women: A World Report, Debbie Taylor, ed. (New York: Oxford University Press, 1985), p. 367.

Table 7
Food, Pregnancy and Infant Mortality

	FOOD (Production as % of requirements in 1981)	ANEMIA (% of pregnant women with anemia)	LOW BIRTH WEIGHT (% babies born weighing under 2500 gm)*	INFANT MORTALITY (% of babies dying in first year of life 1982)
Tanzania	83	59	13	10
Bangladesh	84	66	50	13
Zambia	93	60	14	11
Mali	72	50	13	13
India	86	68	30	9
Zimbabwe	90	27	15	8
Pakistan	106	65	27	12
Indonesia	110	65	18	10
Peru	98	35	9	8
Kenya	88	48	18	8
Papua New Guinea	92	55	25	10
Egypt	116	75	14	10
Colombia	108	22	10	5
Philippines	116	47	11	5
Thailand	105	48	13	5

*5½ pounds.

Source: *Women, A World Report*, Debbie Taylor, ed. (New York: Oxford University Press, 1985), p. 43.

desh, women between the ages of fifteen and forty-five experience an average of eight pregnancies. Such women spend more than half of their adult lives either being pregnant or nursing youngsters. In some cases the intention in having so many children is to ensure that at least some will survive into adulthood. In other cases, the unavailability of contraceptives leaves little alternative. (See Table 8.)

In India in 1980, 90 million married women used no contraception at all. In that country, "it is the teenaged

A young Kenyan woman with her children. The Kenyan government has been trying to promote family planning programs to decrease the number of childbirths.

brides and young mothers who experience the highest maternal mortality rates. The death rate for girls aged 15–19 is almost 50 percent higher than that of their male cohorts, at ages 20–24, almost 80 percent higher . . . Contraceptive pills are virtually unknown and unavailable to poor women in rural areas."[17]

In the many countries that forbid the distribution of contraceptives, information about birth control is difficult to obtain. When abortion is also illegal, or legal only in few instances, women often result to illegal operations,

Table 8
Percentage of Currently Married Women of Child-Bearing Age Using Contraception

Country (or area)	1970	1980
*Afghanistan	2	
*Bangladesh		13
*Barbados		46
Belgium		85
*Benin		18
*Cameroon		2
China		71
*Colombia	21	49
*Costa Rica		66
Czechoslovakia	66	95
Denmark	67	63
*Dominican Republic		42
*Ecuador		34
*Egypt		24
*El Salvador		34
*Fiji	41	
Finland	77	80
France	64	79
*Ghana		10
*Guatemala		18
*Guyana		31
*Haiti		19
*Honduras		27
Hong Kong	42	72
Hungary	67	74
*India	14	
*Indonesia		27
*Iraq	14	
Italy		78
*Jamaica		55
Japan	53	56
*Jordan	22	25
*Kenya	6	8
*Korea (South)	25	58
*Lebanon	53	
*Lesotho		5

Table 8 (Cont.)

Country (or area)	1970	1980
*Malaysia	9	35
Martinique		36
*Mauritania		1
*Mauritius		46
*Mexico		39
*Nepal		7
Netherlands	59	75
*Nigeria		6
*Pakistan	6	3
*Panama		64
*Paraguay		36
*Peru		41
*Philippines	15	39
Poland	60	75
Portugal		66
Puerto Rico	60	69
*Senegal		4
*Singapore	60	71
South Africa		37
Spain		51
*Sri Lanka		55
*Sudan		5
Syria		20
*Thailand	15	59
*Trinidad & Tobago	44	54
*Tunisia		27
*Turkey		38
UK	69	77
USA	65	68
*Venezuela		49
*Yemen, Dem. Rep.		1
*Yemen, Arab Rep.	32	40
Yugoslavia	59	55

*Third World countries (asterisks added by author).

Source: Women: A World Report, Debbie Taylor, ed. (New York: Oxford University Press, 1985), p. 356.

thereby incurring even greater risk to their lives. A world-wide survey of female life in 1980 revealed the following facts:

- 25 percent of all hospital beds in Brazil were filled by women whose illegal abortion attempts had failed.
- abortions accounted for 38 percent of all maternal deaths in Chile
- in Colombia, 66 percent of abortions requiring hospitalization were performed by people with no medical training
- in Thailand, an estimated 10,000 women died annually as a result of illegal abortions
- in Sudan, hospitals reported that illegal abortions were responsible for the majority of gynecological admissions[18]

Sexually Transmitted Disease

AIDS is the sexually transmitted disease most on everyone's mind these days, but there are a host of others which, like AIDS, can affect the health of a fetus. Genital herpes and syphilis, for example, can be transmitted to offspring and result in severe retardation. Women in developing countries are less likely than men to see doctors under any circumstances. But they are especially loathe to go in these cases. They fear being suspected of infidelity, even though their own husbands may have transmitted the disease to them. Some sexually transmitted diseases such as gonorrhea may cause infertility, a common complaint of the Third World women who do go to clinics.

Female Circumcision

In some parts of the world, particularly Africa and the Muslim Middle East, a girl between the ages of six and ten—until the present generation—was customarily subjected to what is known as "female circumcision." Although this practice has largely disappeared in the cities, it hasn't been completely abandoned in rural areas. There are two varieties of the operation. One involves the removal of a part of the clitoris; the other entails the removal of the girl's entire external genitals.

The practice stems from the mistaken belief that if they aren't removed, the female genitals might grow into male external organs. In groups that practice this custom, a husband may react to an uncircumcised bride as if she were the product of a sex-change operation of which he'd been unaware. (In other words, he might believe she had once been a man.) Divorce may follow. Parents also mistakenly believe that without circumcision, their daughters would become oversexed, that their virginity would therefore be even more difficult to monitor, and that their marriageability would thereby be threatened. The psychological effects of the operation on girls are surely considerable but they are difficult to assess given the lack of clinical data. Since it is typically performed by a villager using an unsterilized tool, the procedure can also lead to serious infection. In Kenya, the practice of female circumcision was made illegal by official decree in 1982 following the deaths of fourteen girls.[19]

Occupational Hazards

Third World women also suffer from a variety of illnesses related to the kinds of work they do. Those we met in the rice fields of India, for example, who stand in muddy water all day during the transplanting seasons, are vulnerable to a host of parasitic infections and intestinal troubles. They suffer from severe pain from leech bites, and those who have done this work throughout their adult lives are "permanently bent over and are unable to stand straight at all."[20]

In Bangladesh women agricultural workers complain of

chronic headache and "watering from the eyes and dimness of vision."[21] Women who work in jute production or the textile industry often suffer from an incurable disease called byssinosis. Caused by inhaling fibers and dust particles, it produces breathing difficulties as well as severe chest pain.

For rural people throughout the world, piped water for drinking and household use is an unaccustomed luxury. While it is true that unsanitary water affects the health of both sexes, women in rural communities are under special duress. It is they who traipse to the distant rivers and streams to gather water for their families. There they run the risk of being bitten by the disease-carrying mosquitos, black flies, and tsetse flies that flourish on the banks, and by being infected with bilharzia, a parasitic illness.

In the electronics industry of Southeast Asia, the young women who assemble tiny silicon circuits are wearing glasses by the age of twenty-five as a result of their work. And in South Korea, after one year of employment in the largely female electronics industry, 88 percent of the workers had developed chronic conjunctivitis: inflammation of the membrane that lines the inner surface of the eyelids.[22]

The Problems with Rural Clinics

The American writer and physician Thomas Dooley once noted that being a doctor involves "more than having a knowledge of bugs and drugs". Twenty-five years ago his chief advice to a young colleague about to practice medicine in Southeast Asia was: "Learn how to utilize the fiber and core of your heart."[23]

It is still good advice, but unfortunately it is a tall order in countries where there may be only one health care worker for tens of thousands of people. The human resources of clinics are often severely overtaxed, and a health worker may feel that only a few moments can be spent on a single patient. Not surprisingly, this production line approach to medicine leads many people to cope alone with illness or to consult a traditional village healer with no training in modern medicine. The problem of insufficient health care is by no means limited to countries of the Third World. America's poor also frequently find themselves without the medical benefits available to the more affluent sectors of our society.

Impoverished Third World women cope alone with illness to a greater degree than their menfolk. The reason seems to stem in part from their sense of responsibility. Whether they work as wage laborers or as subsistence farmers, they put in a double shift. For after "work," they fetch water and fuel, prepare meals, and tend children. Lacking anything that might be considered "free time," poor women worldwide typically neglect their illnesses until they are too sick to move.

To make matters worse, rural clinics are frequently located at great distances from home and open only at inconvenient times. Most women will choose to suffer rather than interrupt their work routines to take a long journey. Besides, they know that it will cost money to get there. Often they are dependent on male relatives for the cost of the transportation, or for the transport itself. They may fear rebuff from husbands. In some African groups, it's considered "demeaning" for men to attend clinics with women and children.[24] And in many societies doctors are overwhelmingly men. This is a problem in places where there is a strong feeling that it is improper for women to be examined by men.

Finally, there is usually a large gap in the education and ideas of patients and doctors. Those health workers who don't always strive to "utilize the fiber and core of the heart" often alienate rural patients by dismissing as laughable their ideas about their illness. In poking fun at the

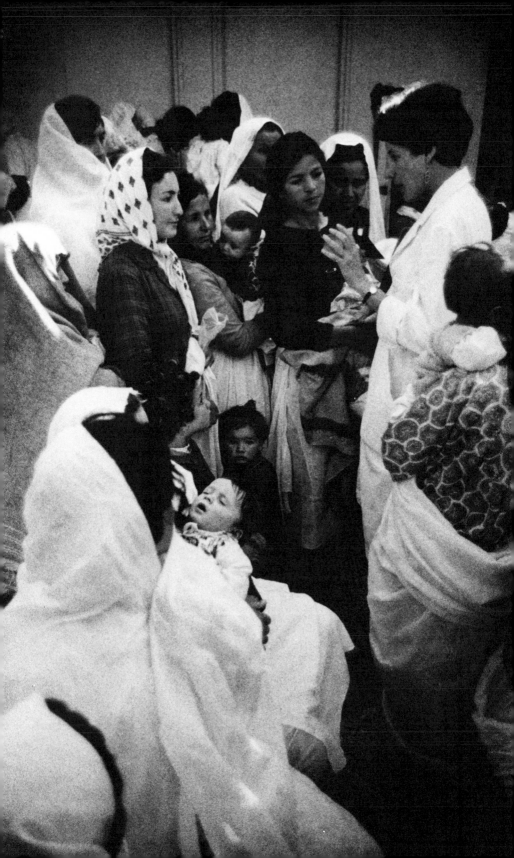

notion of vengeful ghosts or the workings of witches, the Western-trained health worker may cause a patient to go flying back to the traditional village healer.

These healers and herbalists, who are frequently women, increasingly practice in secret, for, lacking licenses, they fear being brought before the law. They service both sexes, but they are particularly important to rural women, who have long depended on them in gynecological matters and during childbirth. Even today women who deliver their babies at home regard the traditional village midwife as a professional, worthy of great respect despite the fact that she is scorned by the medical establishment. Clients are sometimes comforted by the rituals she includes as part of her service, such as burying the placenta in a particular way so as to ensure the health of both mother and infant.

Some writers suggest that rural women of the Third World would be better served if there were an end to the undeclared war waged by the medical profession against the traditional healers and midwives. It would be far better, they say, if doctors and health workers recognized their usefulness, investigated their knowledge, and in order to guarantee the safety of patients, tried to upgrade their skills. At the very least, traditional healers could be given training in the practice of sanitary techniques.

The Good News

In September 1978, 134 nations participated in the International Conference on Primary Health Care held in Alma Ata, in the Soviet Union. The motto of the conference was:

Health care workers, like this one in a family planning clinic in Tunisia, often face crowded, difficult working conditions.

"Health for all by the year 2000." There are still many giant steps to be taken before this goal can be reached. But an encouraging number of baby steps have already moved the world in the right direction. Many of these will improve the health of women in particular.

In Indonesia, Malaysia, and the Philippines, where the majority of women now have access to family planning and fertility information services, the birth rate has been substantially reduced. Such family planning services, however, are not without problems. They may unwittingly promote unsafe methods of contraception. For example, Depo Provera was regarded in 1967 as a safe, effective contraceptive and was distributed widely in Third World

A Costa Rican doctor and her patient discuss family planning.

countries. But research conducted in the 1970s suggested that the drug might be cancer-producing and its use was therefore banned in the United States. Yet some countries still permit use of the controversial drug. In Thailand alone, 86,000 women had already been injected.[25]

The unambiguously good news is that in Guatemala, where impoverished pregnant women are now given supplementary food under the auspices of the government, the incidence of low birth weight among babies has been reduced by 25 percent.[26] And in 1978, the Jamaica Woman's Bureau established the first counseling service for adolescent mothers in the developing world. It allows teen mothers to continue their required education while receiving postnatal care. In Latin America, where cancer of the cervix is the most common form of cancer among women, the Pan American Health Organization is attempting to get health officials from eighteen countries to agree to collect women's health data, including violence against women and the occupational aspects of their health.

In some places women have finally been given a public voice in matters that affect health. Costa Rica now ensures equal participation of the sexes in community planning and the evaluation of local health services.

In 1985, the Philippine Ministry of Health linked up with the National Federation of Women's Clubs, an organization with a membership of 300,000 Philippine women in 76 provinces and 65 cities. The aim was to encourage women to identify the particular health needs of their communities. An example of one success story is that of a Mother's Club in Surigao City.

The group determined that its number-one priority ought to be making safe drinking water available on a regular basis. As in so many places, neighborhood women had to travel from three to five kilometers to obtain household water. As a result of their lobbying efforts, the raw materials for a piped water system—pipes, fittings, and tools—finally arrived. Then the women enlisted the neighborhood residents—male and female alike—to contribute their labor. The project took twelve weeks to complete, but now the community has drinkable water within easy reach. In a short time a decline was noted in the incidence of gastroenteritis, an inflammation of the stomach and intestines caused by impure water.

The funding for most of these health projects necessarily comes from the governments of Third World and other countries. But private organizations, such as the International Women's Health Coalition, based in New York City, also give assistance to women of developing nations. This group in particular is concerned with providing "high quality reproductive health care." This includes pregnancy testing and making health care services readily available to new mothers. Training projects are already under way in Bangladesh, Indonesia, and the Philippines, and there are plans for others in Brazil, the Caribbean, and Africa.

BECOMING AN
EQUAL CITIZEN

On a spring day in 1983 some of us gathered to protest the new government's insistence that we women wear the *chador*, the headdress Iranian women wear to veil themselves. Suddenly I noticed among us one obviously pregnant woman who was herself wearing a *chador*. I felt compelled to ask her: "Do you realize where you are? This is a protest against the *chador*." "I know," she replied. "It is too late for me, but it is not for myself that I am here. I am carrying a baby, and if it is a daughter I want her to have a clear choice as to whether she wears it or not." A jeering ring of observers soon closed in on us and began to throw stones at us. There was no way to prevent what happened in the minutes that followed. This woman was hit and fell down. I later learned that she lost the baby, a daughter as it turned out.[1]

In Iran "as of April 1983, the wearing of the *chador* was made compulsory for all women; the penalty for going unveiled is a 1 month–1 year imprisonment."[2]

Even something we take as much for granted as the choice of clothing we wear when we step outside our front door is in some places a right that women must still fight for. Like so many things—a fair chance at getting an elementary, high school, and college education and equal access to health facilities, credit lines, job opportunities, and public office—this right is bound up with national as well as household politics.

A group of Iranian women display a variety
of emotions while wearing the chaldor.

The International Women's Movement

The feminist movement of the 1970s, and particularly the U.N. Conferences on Women held in 1975 and 1980, spurred the political organization of women at the national level throughout the Third World. In 1978, for example, "the first steps were taken toward forming the organization that was to become AMES (the Association of Salvadoran Women) as a way of incorporating into political life those sectors of women (housewives, professionals, teachers, secretaries, shantytown dwellers, students, etc.) who, because of their special circumstances, had not yet joined the people's struggle."[3]

The new feminism even resulted in an organization of women that transcended national boundaries. The First Meeting of Latin American and Caribbean Women addressed itself to the need for research on women and for the denunciation of different forms of violence against women. This meeting led to the formation in 1981 of the Latin American and Caribbean Association for the Study of Women, with headquarters in Brazil.

A Fijian woman who attended the international conference of women held in Mexico City in the summer of 1975 writes: "Mexico City was important . . . for the increased awareness it gave Pacific women of the multiplicity of interests that made up the international women's movement. . . . What Mexico revealed to Pacific women, and to women generally, was the movement itself. There *was* a women's movement and it was worldwide; it wasn't just American, or British, or white, as the media had painted it."[4]

Among the issues that most concern Pacific island women are: the use, by industrial countries, of the Pacific islands as a dumping ground for nuclear waste and the exploitation of Pacific island women by the tourist industries. Through newly established regional organization their protesting voices are finally being heard by the appropriate commissions. But there is a long way to go in these areas of concern and in others which the women share with feminists around the world. There are in the Pacific, according to one Fijian feminist, "still too many women who will not be able to use contraceptives because their husbands have told them not to, too many girls who will not finish school because they are pregnant, too many women who cannot conceive of leaving bad marriages because it is simply not done. We have not dealt with the personal powerlessness that many women face."[5]

In some Third World countries, the current rise in women's status is due not specifically to the international women's movement but stems from another source—war. Some governments have had to recognize that in part their rise to power is due to the participation of women in recent civil wars. An example is Nicaragua.

The Women Warriors

Discovered by Christopher Columbus in 1502 and ruled for three centuries from abroad, Nicaragua became in 1821 part of a political entity newly independent from Spain— the United Provinces of Central America. Seventeen years later Nicaragua declared itself independent from the United Provinces. Since then the country has had nine written constitutions. For the past half century Nicaraguans have sought to overthrow successive dictatorships. In 1979, a revolution led by the Sandinista National Liberation Front (FSLN) ousted Anastasio Somoza, then the ruler. At that time it is estimated that the Somoza family controlled as much as 40 percent of the country's economy.[6]

The Nicaraguan revolution was one waged by the young, but among those above the age of thirty-five, "women's participation seems to far surpass that of men. . . . Women fought in the front lines as FSLN militants, participated in support tasks, worked under cover in government offices, and were involved in every facet of the anti-Somoza opposition movement. They built a broadly based organization of women, the Association of Nicaraguan Women Confronting the Nation's Problems (AMPRONAC), which itself played a key role in organizing against the dictatorship. By the final offensive, women made up 30 percent of the Sandinista army and held important leadership positions, commanding everything from small units to full battalions."[7]

Nicaraguan women were motivated to take an active role in the revolution because of their outrage at the government's treatment of children. Hearing of eight- and nine-year olds being assassinated for collecting money for the Sandinistas or for speaking out against Somoza in school, these women became committed foes of the government. They responded by mobilizing people against Somoza; they also organized food supply depots for the Sandinista army and provided medicine for their wounded.

Women who led such activities rose to positions of power after the coup. Lea Guido, for instance, an early leader of AMPRONAC, became the minister of the Ministry of Social Welfare in the Sandinista government and an ardent speaker for women's equality. She was succeeded by Maria Lourdes Vargas in 1983. In that year 48 percent of government officials were women.[8] AMPRONAC, renamed the Luisa Amanda Espinoza Association of Nicaraguan Women (AMNLAE) in honor of the first woman to die in combat in the 1979 revolution, is the official state women's organization. In 1983 AMNLAE, in conjunction with the International Labor Organization and the International Metalworkers Federation, was active in the free-trade zones of the capital city, Managua, organizing female employees in labor-intensive industries. In the same year it helped to organize Nicaraguan female agricultural workers. The association has also been responsible for creating more government-sponsored day-care centers for children of working mothers. Unfortunately, peace did not last long in Nicaragua. In 1985, the new government under President Daniel Ortega decreed a state of emergency with the result that civil rights relating to the judicial process have been suspended. From that same year civil war has continued to the time of writing, with heavy combat in the northern region of the country resulting in more than 14,000 deaths to date.[9] But if the past is any guide, the country's women will continue to be central to the governance of Nicaragua.

Women in Political Office

Ancient Egypt occasionally experienced leadership by powerful women: Queen Hatshepsut, who maintained peace during her eighteen-year reign; Queen Nefertiti, a brilliant stateswoman who ruled along with Akhnaten; and, of course, Queen Cleopatra. Today, Egyptian women with political aspirations face a situation that is both more and less encouraging.

On the one hand, in that country "women are prevented from holding certain high-level positions, such as provincial governor" and "because of a reading of Islamic law, a woman's testimony is considered worth half a man's, which prevents women from holding judgeships."[10] At the cabinet level, women have occupied only one position, that of minister of social affairs. In 1982, the Egyptian feminist writer Nawal El Saadawi organized a pan-Arab women's rights association which was to have its headquarters in Egypt. In 1983, "the Association was refused registration as an organization by the Egyptian government."[11]

On the other hand, the Egyptian constitution was amended in 1979 to create a Parliament with thirty seats reserved for women, including one for each governing district. In 1982, forty-two women were serving in Parlia-

Nicaragua's Ambassador to the United Nations, Nora
Astorga, listens to arguments over U.S. aid to her
country at a UN Security Council meeting in 1986.

Table 9
Membership of National Legislative Bodies

Country (or area)	1970 M	1970 F	1980 M	1980 F
Australia	187	4	170	19
Austria	213	23	206	30
*Barbados	23	1	26	1
Belgium	368	26	360	34
Bulgaria	322	78	317	83
*Burundi			59	6
Byelorussia	271	159	305	130
Canada	360	15	343	39
*Chile	185	15	77	3
China	2,232	653	2,346	632
*Costa Rica	55	5	55	4
*Cuba	376	105	386	113
Cyprus	35	0	34	1
Czechoslovakia	251	99	251	99
Denmark	149	30	137	42
*Dominica	20	1	20	1
*Dominican Republic	103	15	139	8
*Ecuador			134	4
*Egypt			615	43
*El Salvador			50	10
*Equatorial Guinea			58	2
Finland	154	46	138	62
France			770	38
Germany (East)	332	168	338	162
Germany (West)	480	38	469	51
Greece	293	7	286	14
*Guyana	44	9	55	16
*Honduras			76	6
Hungary	251	101	243	109
Iceland	57	3	51	9
*India	523	19	514	28
*Indonesia	429	31	418	42
Ireland	197	11	206	20
Israel	112	8	112	8
Italy	928	23	886	66
*Ivory Coast	99	11	139	8
Japan	701	25	733	26

Table 9 (Cont.)

Country	1970		1980	
(or area)	M	F	M	F
*Kenya	168	4	169	3
*Korea (South)	213	8	268	8
Luxembourg	56	3	53	6
*Malawi	83	4	96	10
*Malaysia	148	6	146	8
*Mauritius	67	3	66	4
*Mexico			110	54
Mongolia			77	23
*Nepal			128	7
Netherlands	202	23	182	43
New Zealand	83	4	84	8
Norway	131	24	115	40
*Philippines	166	12	165	7
Poland	365	95	346	114
Portugal	230	20	232	18
Romania	275	66	247	122
*Rwanda			61	9
*Saint Lucia	18	2	26	2
Samoa	46	1	46	1
*Senegal	92	8	107	13
Spain	800	27	571	32
*Sri Lanka	161	6	147	7
Sweden	274	75	251	98
Switzerland	229	15	221	25
*Turkey	627	7	387	12
UK	1,715	75	1,762	87
Ukraine SSR			416	234
*Uruguay	96	3		
USA	516	19	511	23
USSR	1,025	475	1,008	492
*Venezuela			219	12
*Vietnam	358	132	389	106
Yugoslavia	86	13	83	17
*Zambia	127	8	131	4
*Zimbabwe			122	11

*Third World countries (asterisks added by author).

Source: *Women: A World Report,* Debbie Taylor, ed. (New York: Oxford University Press, 1985), p. 375.

ment, having either been elected in contests against male candidates or appointed by the country's president to fill a reserved seat.[12] Three-quarters of the female Parliamentarians had received university degrees; a quarter of them had graduate degrees, frequently from prestigious schools in the West. In general, their overall level of education was higher than that of their male colleagues. Most were married and had had children. None of these women had begun her professional life in politics. At the time of their election or appointment they were typically in their forties and had already spent between five and twenty years at a successful career in education, journalism, or the mass media. Quite naturally, these women represent a range of political beliefs, but on one issue they are united. That is the effort to liberalize the nation's Personal Status Laws, those laws which, rooted in the Koran, today govern Egyptian marriage, divorce, and child custody.

Elsewhere around the world women are gaining access to high-level government posts where they have not been represented before, at least in modern times. (See Table 9). In 1984 in Ghana, Nigeria, Senegal, Zambia, and Zimbabwe, women were holding cabinet positions. Burkina Faso (formerly Upper Volta) has five women ministers as well as many female high commissioners and directors of departments. Josephine Quédraogo is the nation's minister of family affairs. In 1986, in an interview by journalist Margaret Novicki, she had this to say about the current state of the "war between men and women" in her country and what she hoped to do about it:

> When women have an opportunity to speak out, they tell us: "Men regard us solely as baby [making] machines. As soon as you are pregnant, the men are satisfied and they ask nothing more of you."
>
> There has been a rupture in relations between men and women in the household. Our priority in this ministry is to have the woman accepted as a person with opinions about her life, her relationship with her husband, and the education of her family . . . to raise the personal economic status of women. . . . If women

don't have access to an income today, it is probably because they have to spend too much time on their domestic responsibilities, and these must be eased.[13]

In Latin America, holding high office has historically been a male prerogative. Even in 1984, Brazil, Peru, Ecuador, Chile, and Argentina had between them only two female ministers. In Brazil, however, between 1972 and 1976, sixty women were elected as mayors.[14] The number sounds high, but in fact it represents only a tiny percentage of the mayors elected. A study conducted on this group showed that it was not the big, industrial Brazilian cities that elected female mayors, but the smaller, more rural municipalities in which many men had been forced to leave to find work elsewhere. In short, they were towns with a highly skewed sex ratio in their populations.

As in Egypt, a major difference between female office-holders and their male counterparts is that they are relatively new to politics. Men generally came to office with previous experience in politics; the women came with prior experience as teachers or social welfare workers. Many had to fight family objections that they could not fulfill their domestic responsibilities while being mayor. Those who succeeded in being elected then found they had a double fight on their hands: the protests of their family against their frequent need to make trips alone to the capital where they had to fight for limited federal resources to improve the roads, schools, and sanitation facilities of their home town!

EPILOGUE

It is hard not to become angry when one considers the historical prejudice against females in such areas as health care, nutrition, education, and in the most desirable occupations. It is harder still to bear silent witness to that prejudice today. As we have seen, in the Third World the opportunities for attaining some measure of control over one's destiny have, until very recently, been vastly unequal for the two sexes. Today in many countries the status of womankind is improving. But sadly there are also places, such as Iran with its strictly enforced dress code, where women are losing ground in their struggle for equality.

Finally on the issue of women's status the Third World is not completely a world apart. In rich countries as well as poor, women suffer acts of sexual violence. Even in the United States, according to a world survey, as many as a quarter of reported crimes involve assault on wives.[1] In rich and poor countries alike, women put in less time than men at paying jobs while they spend many more hours doing unpaid labor. And statistics reveal that in the West women are less likely than men to have high-paying, prestigious jobs and more likely than men to care for their aging parents. In Great Britain, for example, an estimated

300,000 women remain unmarried and childless in order to do so.[2]

However, in the Third World the situation is more dire. There, the greatest hope for the future lies in improved educational opportunities for girls and women—not the kind of education that puts effective limits on their aspirations, but rather the kind that says: "You can do anything!"

NOTES

Chapter 2: Being Born Female

1. Emrys Peters, "The Status of Women in Four Middle Eastern Communities," in *Women in the Muslim World*, ed. Lois Beck and Nikki Keddie (Cambridge, Mass.: Harvard University Press, 1978), 314.

2. Doranne Jacobson, "The Women of North and Central India," in *Women in India: Two Perspectives*, Doranne Jacobson and Susan Wadley (Columbia, Mo.: South Asia Books, 1977), 33.

3. Sudhir Kakar, *The Inner World: A Psychoanalytic Study of Childhood and Society in India* (New Delhi: Oxford University Press, 1978), 57.

4. Leigh Minturn, *The Rajputs of Khalapur* (New York: John Wiley, 1966), 97.

5. Amartya Sen and Sunil Sengputa, "Malnutrition and Rural Children and the Sex Bias," *Economic and Political Weekly* (May 1983): 857.

6. Nawal El Saadawi, *The Hidden Face of Eve* (London: Zed Press, 1980).

Chapter 3: Growing Up

1. Ali Ghalem, *A Wife For My Son*, trans. G. Kazolias (Chicago: Banner Press, 1984), 124.

2. Fatma Mansur Cosar, "Women in Turkish Society," in *Women in the Muslim World*, ed. Lois Beck and Nikki Keddie (Cambridge, Mass.: Harvard University Press, 1978), 126.

3. Debbie Taylor, ed., *Women: A World Report* (New York: Oxford University Press, 1985), 11.

4. The following section summarizes information in the article by Dawn Chatty, "Changing Sex Roles in Bedouin Society," in Beck and Keddie, 399–415.

5. Robin Morgan, "Good News from 18 Countries: Small Steps For Womankind," *Ms.* (Sept. 1985): 12.

6. Chatty, 407.

7. Doranne Jacobson, "The Women of North and Central India," in *Women In India: Two Perspectives,* Doranne Jacobson and Susan Wadley (Columbia, Mo.: South Asia Books, 1977), 35.

8. Manisha Roy, *Bengali Women* (Chicago: University of Chicago Press, 1975), 37.

9. George Thomas Kurian, ed., *Encyclopoedia of the Third World* (New York: Facts on File, 1986), 665.

10. Kurian, 680.

Chapter 4: Getting An Education

1. The discussion on Kuwaiti education is based on the article by Kamala Nath, "Education and Employment among Kuwaiti Women," in *Women in the Muslim World,* ed. Lois Beck and Nikki Keddie (Cambridge, Mass.: Harvard University Press, 1978), 172–188.

2. Nath, 177.

3. Robin Morgan ed., *Sisterhood Is Global* (New York: Doubleday, Anchor Press, 1984), 324.

4. Morgan, 582.

5. Morgan, 582.

6. Morgan, 324.

7. Morgan, 525.

8. This discussion is based on the article by Karen Coffyn Biraimah, "The Impact of Western Schools on Girls' Expectations: A Togolese Case," in *Women's Education in the Third World: Comparative Perspectives,* ed. Gail P. Kelly and Carolyn M. Elliott (Albany: The State University of New York Press, 1982), 188–202.

9. Biraimah, p. 193.

10. Education Commission, India. *Recommendations on Women's Education.* (New Delhi: Education Commission, 1965), 5.

11. The following discussion is drawn from the article by Narenda Nath Kalia, "Images of Men and Women in Indian Textbooks," in Kelly and Elliott, 173–187.

12. Kalia, 175.

13. Kalia, 180.

14. The following statistics are drawn from the study by Catalina H. Wainerman, "The Impact of Education on the Labor Force in Argentina and Paraguay," in Kelly and Elliott, 264–279.

15. Wainerman, 267.

16. E. Schiefelbein and J. Farrell, "Women, Schooling, and Work in Chile," in Kelly and Elliott, 228–248.

17. Audrey Chapman Smock, *Women's Education in Developing*

Countries: Opportunities and Outcomes (New York: Praeger, 1981), 253.

Chapter 5: Marriage and Motherhood

1. Doranne Jacobson, "The Women of North and Central India," in *Women in India: Two Perspectives,* Doranne Jacobson and Susan Wadley (Columbia, Mo.: South Asia Books, 1977), 46.
2. Manisha Roy, *Bengali Women* (Chicago: University of Chicago Press, 1975), 79.
3. Roy, p. 78.
4. Madhav S. Gore, "The Husband-Wife, Mother-Son Relationship," *Sociological Bulletin* 11 (1961): 91–102.
5. Sudhir Kakar, *The Inner World: A Psycho-Analytic Study of Childhood and Society in India* (New Delhi: Oxford University Press, 1978), 77.
6. Roy, 125.
7. Margaret Cormack, *The Hindu Women* (Westport, Conn.: Greenwood Press, 1975), 151.
8. Jacobson, 77.
9. Kakar, 79.
10. The following discussion is drawn from the article by Noel Coulson and Doreen Hinchcliffe, "Women and Law Reform in Contemporary Islam," in *Women in the Muslim World,* ed. Lois Beck and Nikki Keddie (Cambridge, Mass.: Harvard University Press, 1978), 37–51.
11. Elizabeth H. White, "Legal Reform as an Indicator of Women's Status in Muslim Nations," in Beck and Keddie, 58.
12. Coulson and Hinchcliffe, 45
13. Alice Hellyer Dally, *The Chief* (Ibadan, Nigeria: African Universities Press, 1984), 180.
14. Claire C. Robertson, *Sharing The Same Bowl* (Bloomington, Indiana: Indiana University Press, 1984), 180.
15. Robertson, 185.
16. Christine Oppong, *Marriage Among A Matrilineal Elite: A Family Study Of Ghanaian Civil Servants.* (Cambridge: Cambridge University Press, 1974), 65.
17. Oppong, 75–76.
18. Robertson, 182.
19. Margaret Strobel, "African Women," *Signs* 8, no. 1, (1982): 116.
20. Robertson, 198.

Chapter 6: On The Land

1. The profile of Fanisi Kalusa is drawn from the article by John Tierney, "Fanisi's Choice," *Science 86* (Jan.–Feb. 1986): 26–42.

2. Debbie Taylor, *Women: A World Report* (New York: Oxford University Press, 1985), 16.

3. Shezue Tomaoda, "Measuring Female Labour Activities in Asian Developing Countries: A Time-Allocation Approach," *International Labour Review* 24, no. 6 (Nov.–Dec. 1985): 662.

4. Taylor, 17.

5. Gary Whitby, "Successfully Processing Sorghum," *Appropriate Technology* 12, no. 1 (n.d.).

6. Ann Stoler, "Class Structures and Female Autonomy in Rural Java," *Signs* 3, no. 1,: 87.

7 Lala Gulati, "Agricultural Laborers," in *Women and Work in India,* ed. J. Libra, J. Paulson, and J. Everett (New Delhi: Promilla, 1984), 63–76.

8. Taylor, 18.

9. Robin Morgan, *Sisterhood Is Global* (New York: Doubleday, Anchor Press, 1984), 314.

10. "World Survey: Women in Agriculture," (Nairobi, Kenya, 1985). Proceedings of a Conference to Appraise the Achievements of the UN Decade For Women.

11. "The State of the World's Women: 1985" (Nairobi, Kenya, 1985), 7.

12. "The State of the World's Women: 1985" (Nairobi, Kenya, 1985), 9.

Chapter 7: Women In Industry

1. Information in this section comes from the article by Emily DiCicco and Deborah Ziska, "Factory Wages," *Americas* (Sept.–Oct. 1985): 33–36.

2. DiCicco and Ziska, 35.

3. Debbie Taylor, *Women: A World Report* (New York: Oxford University Press, 1985), 46.

4. Barbara Ehrenreich and Annette Fuentes, "Life On The Global Assembly Line," *Ms.* (Jan. 1981): 55.

5. Taylor, 39.

6. Robin Morgan, *Sisterhood Is Global* (New York: Doubleday, Anchor Press, 1984), 312.

7. Ehrenreich and Fuentes, 55.

8. Iris Berger, "Sources of Class Consciousness: South African Women in Recent Labor Struggles," in *Women and Class in Africa,* ed. Claire Robertson and Iris Berger (New York: Africana Publishing Company, 1986), 216–237.

9. Taylor, 39.

10. Ehrenreich and Fuentes, 55.

11. Linda Y. C. Lim, "Capitalism, Imperialism, and Patriarch: The Dilemma of Third World Workers in Multinational Factories," in *Women, Men, and the International Division of Labor,* ed. June Nash and Maria Patricia Fernandez Kelly (Albany, N.Y.: The State University of New York Press, 1984), 74.

12. UNCT/ILO, "Women Workers in Multinational Enterprises in Developing Countries" (Geneva: International Labor Office, 1985), 7.

13. Lourdes Arizpe and Josefina Aranda, "The 'Comparative Advantages' and Women's Disadvantages in the Strawberry Export Agribusiness in Mexico," *Signs* 7, no. 2, (1981): 460.

14. UNCT/ILO, 31.

15. Taylor, 32.

16. Taylor, 32.

17. Taylor, 32.

Chapter 8: Being In Business

1. Debbie Taylor, *Women: A World Report* (New York: Oxford University Press, 1985), 40.

2. Dan Aronson, *The City Is Our Farm* (Cambridge, Mass.: Schenkman Publishing Co., 1978).

3. The description of market women in Lima is drawn from Ximena Bunster B.'s article, "Market Sellers in Lima, Peru," in *Women and Poverty in the Third World,* M. Buvinic, M. Lycette, and W. Paul McGreevey (Baltimore, Maryland: The Johns Hopkins University Press, 1983), 92–103.

4. Kanitha Srisilpavongsa, "Sex Makes No Difference," *Business in Thailand* (Feb. 1983): 84–89.

5. James Guyot, "The Role of Women in Thailand's Managerial Revolution," (Ann Arbor, Mich.: University of Michigan Southeast Asia Institute of Summer Studies, 1985).

6. Guyot.

7. Earl Sullivan, *Women in Egyptian Public Life* (Syracuse, N.Y.: Syracuse University Press, 1986), 133.

8. Robin Morgan, *Sisterhood Is Global* (New York: Doubleday, Anchor Press, 1984), 698.

9. Sullivan, 139.

10. Sullivan, 146.

11. Sullivan, 152.

12. Elanga Shungu, "Africa's Mercedes Ladies," *World Press Review* (Jan. 1985): 52.

13. Author interview

Chapter 9: Entering The Professions

1. Author interview

2. George Thomas Kurian, ed. *Encyclopedia of the Third World* (New York: Facts On File, 1986).

3. David Finkelstein, "Korea's 'Quiet' Revolutionary," *The Christian Century* (April 1981): 483–85.

4. Robin Morgan, *Sisterhood is Global* (New York: Doubleday, Anchor Press, 1984), 403.

Chapter 10: Getting Health Care

1. Banoo J. Coyati, "India: Women's Deteriorating Health," in *Health Needs of the World's Poor Women,* ed. Patricia Blair (Washington, D.C.: Equity Policy Center, 1981), 3.

2. Zafrullah Chwodhury, "A Double Oppression in Bangladesh," in Blair, 5.

3. Coyati, 12.

4. Debbie Taylor, *Women: A World Report* (New York: Oxford University Press, 1985), 46.

5. Belkes Wolde Giorgis, "Africa: Health Requires Economic Advancement for Women," in Blair, 15.

6. Taylor, 43.

7. Coyati, 3.

8. Prabha Ramalingaswami, "Maternal and Post Partum Health in India," in Blair, 26.

9. Chowdhury, 5.

10. International Fertility Research Program, *Reproductive Age Mortality Survey* (North Carolina: Research Triangle Park, 1980).

11. Taylor, p. 43.

12. Celia Ferrera Santos, "Brazil: The Health Implications of Urban Pauperism," in Blair, 26.

13. Taylor, 43.

14. William Chandler, "Primary Care in the Gambia," *Natural History* (April 1986): 66.

15. Nonceba Lubanga, "South Africa: Health and the Effects of the Political System," in Blair, 16.

16. Jose Villar and Jose Belizan, "Women's Poor Health in Developing Countries: A Vicious Cycle," in Blair, 39.

17. Kaval Gulhati, "Women-to-Women Delivery Systems For Family Planning," in Blair, 83.

18. Robin Morgan, *Sisterhood Is Global* (New York: Doubleday, Anchor Press, 1984).

19. Morgan, 393.

20. Joan Mencher and K. Saradamoni, "Muddy Feet, Dirty Hands: Rice Production and Female Agricultural Labor," *Economic and Political Weekly* (Dec. 1982): 153.

21. Chowdury, 4.

22. Barbara Ehrenreich and Annette Fuentes, "Life on the Global Assembly Line," *Ms.* (Jan. 1981): 56.

23. Agnes Dooley, *Promises To Keep* (New York: Farrar, Straus and Cudahy, 1962), 265.

24. Douglas Lackey, "Practice Versus Theory in Primitive Health Care in East Africa," in Blair, 73.

25. Marjorie Sun, "Depo Provera Revs Up At F.D.A.," *Science* (July 30, 1982).

26. The "good news" reported for the Caribbean and Latin America is from Shushum Bhotie, "Status and Survival," *World Health* (April 1985): 12–15.

Chapter 11: Becoming an Equal Citizen

1. Personal communication

2. Robin Morgan, ed. *Sisterhood Is Global* (New York: Doubleday, Anchor Press, 1984), 327.

3. Association of Salvadoran Women, "El Salvador: 'We Cannot Wait'," trans. Bobbye Ortiz, in *Sisterhood Is Global*, ed. Robin Morgan (New York: Doubleday, Anchor Press, 1984), 210.

4. Vanessa Griffen, "The Pacific Islands: All It Requires Is Ourselves," in Morgan, 517.

5. Griffen, 522.

6. Margaret Randall, *Sandino's Daughters* (Vancouver: New Star Books, 1981), 4.

7. George Thomas Kurian, ed. *Encyclopedia of the Third World* (New York: Facts on File, 1986), 14.

8. Morgan, 485.

9. Kurian, 1439.

10. Morgan, 194.

11. Morgan, 199.

12. Earl Sullivan, *Women in Egyptian Public Life* (Syracuse, N.Y.: University of Syracuse Press, 1986).

13. Margaret Novicki, "Josephine Quédraogo, Minister of Family Affairs, Burkina Faso," *African Report* (Nov.–Dec. 1986): 26–30.

14. Eva Alterman Blay, "The Political Participation of Women in Brazil," trans. Susan A. Soleiro, *Signs* 5 (1979): 42–59.

Epilogue

1. Debbie Taylor, ed. *Women: A World Report* (New York: Oxford University Press, 1985), 64.

2. Taylor, 15.

FURTHER READING

Agarwal, Bina. "Women, Poverty, and Agricultural Growth in India." *Journal of Peasant Studies* 13, 4 (1986): 165–218.

Beck, Lois, and Keddie, Nikki, eds. *Women in the Muslim World.* Cambridge, Mass.: Harvard University Press, 1978.

Blair, Patricia, ed. *Health Needs of the World's Poor Women.* Washington, D.C.: Equity Policy Center, 1981.

Boserup, Ester. *Women's Role in Economic Development.* New York: St. Martin's Press, 1970.

Buvinic M., Lycette, M., and McGreevey, William Paul, eds. *Women and Poverty in the Third World.* Baltimore, Md.: The Johns Hopkins University Press, 1983.

Dally, Alice Hellyer. *The Chief.* Ibadan, Nigeria: African Universities Press, 1982.

De Souza, Alfred, ed. *Women in Contemporary India and Southeast Asia.* New Delhi: Ashokas Press, 1980.

Duley, Margot, and Edwards, Mary, eds. *The Cross-Cultural Study of Women.* New York: The Feminist Press, 1986.

Ehrenreich, Barbara, and Fuentes, Annette. "Life on the Global Assembly Line." *Ms.* (Jan. 1981): 52–59.

Emechita, Buchi. *Second Class Citizen.* New York: George Braziller, 1975.

Fernea, Elizabeth. "Women and Family in Development Plans in the Arab East." *Journal of Asian and African Studies* 21 (1986): 81–88.

Ghalem, Ali. *A Wife For My Son.* Translated by G. Kazolias. Chicago: Banner Press, 1984.

Hay, Margaret, and Stichter, Sharon. *African Women South of the Sahara.* New York: Longman, 1984.

Islam, Shada. "Third World Women." *Women Press Review* (June 1980): 39–44.

Jacobson, Doranne. "The Women of North and Central India." In *Women in India: Two Perspectives*. Doranne Jacobson and Susan Wadley. Columbia, Mo.: South Asia Books, 1977.

Kelly, Gail P., and Elliott, Carolyn M., eds. *Women's Education in the Third World: Comparative Perspectives*. Albany, N.Y.: State University of New York Press, 1982.

Libra, J., Paulson, J., and Everett, J. *Women and Work in India*. New Delhi: Promilla and Company, 1984.

Lim, Linda Y. C. "Capitalism, Imperialism, and Patriarchy: The Dilemma of Third World Workers in Multinational Factories." In *Women, Men, and the International Division of Labor*, edited by June Nash and Maria Patricia Fernandez Kelly. Albany, N.Y.: State University of New York Press, 1984.

Mencher, Joan, and Saradamoni, K. "Muddy Feet, Dirty Hands: Rice Production and Female Agricultural Labor." *Economic and Political Weekly* (Dec. 1982): 149–167.

Morgan, Robin, ed. *Sisterhood Is Global*. New York: Doubleday, Anchor Press, 1984.

Mujica, Barbara. "Women in Transition." *Americas* (Sept.–Oct. 1985): 24–28.

Njoku, John E. *The World of the African Woman*. Metuchen, N.J.: Scarecrow, 1980.

O'Barr, Jean, ed. *Third World Women*. Chapel Hill, N.C.: Duke University Press, 1976.

Robertson, Claire C. *Sharing The Same Bowl*. Bloomington, Ind.: Indiana University Press, 1984.

Roy, Manisha. *Bengali Women*. Chicago: University of Chicago Press, 1975.

Saunders, Lucie Wood, and McKenna, Sohair. "Unseen Hands: Women's Farm Work in an Egyptian Village." *Anthropological Quarterly* 59, no. 3 (1986): 105–114.

Sen, Amartya, and Sengupta, Sunil. "Malnutrition and Rural Children and the Sex Bias." *Economic and Political Weekly* (May 1983).

Smock, Audrey Chapman. *Women's Education in Developing Countries: Opportunities and Outcomes*. New York: Praeger, 1981.

Strobel, Margaret. "African Women." *Signs* 8, no. 1 (1982): 109–131.

Sullivan, Earl. *Women in Egyptian Public Life*, Syracuse, N.Y.: Syracuse University Press, 1986.

Taylor, Debbie, ed. *Women: A World Report*. New York: Oxford University Press, 1985.

INDEX

305.4
FIS
  Fisher, Maxine P.
  Women in the
  Third World

13,125

305.4
FIS
  Fisher, Maxine P.
  Women in the
  Third World

13,125

DATE DUE	BORROWER'S NAME